Providing Reference Services for Archives and Manuscripts

by Mary Jo Pugh

The Society of American Archivists

Chicago

1992

∞ *Providing Reference Services for Archives and Manuscripts* is printed on alkaline, acid-free printing paper manufactured with no groundwood pulp. As such, it substantially meets the requirements of the American National Standards Institute—Permanence of Paper for Printed Library Materials, ANSI 239.48-1984. Typesetting and printing of this publication is done by Port City Press of Baltimore, Maryland. Manufactured in the United States.

ISBN 0-931828-82-1

TABLE OF CONTENTS

Preface / 1

Acknowledgments / 2

Chapter 1   **Reference Services in Archives / 3**
- Origin and Diversity of Archives / 3
- Rationales for Archives / 4
- Historical Developments in the Use of Archives / 4
- Access to Archives / 6
- Reference Services in Archives / 6
- Ethics of Reference Services / 8
- Promoting the Use of Archives / 9
- Goals of this Manual / 9

Chapter 2   **Identifying Users of Archives / 11**
- The Values of Archives / 11
- Uses of Archives / 12
- Identifying Individual Needs / 13
- Identifying Services and Programs for User Groups / 14

Chapter 3   **Providing Intellectual Access / 25**
- Information about Repositories / 25
- Information about Holdings / 28
- Information from Holdings / 35
- Information about Records Creators / 38
- Referrals / 38

Chapter 4   **The Reference Process / 41**
- Reference Interaction / 41
- Telephone and Mail Inquiries / 49
- Public Programs / 50

Chapter 5   **Determining Access Policies / 55**
- Reference and Access / 55
- Defining Access Policies / 59

Chapter 6   **Providing Physical Access / 65**
- Security / 65
- Preservation / 66
- Reference Facilities / 68
- Policies for Use / 70
- Automation of Registration and Retrieval Procedures / 76
- Reference Policies for Electronic Records / 76

Chapter 7   **Copies and Loans** / 79
- Copying / 79
- Types of Copies / 80
- Copyright / 81
- Repository Copying Policies and Procedures / 85
- Providing Original Documents on Loan / 89
- Loan Policies and Procedures / 90

Chapter 8   **Managing Reference Services and Evaluating the Use of Archives** / 93
- Organizing Reference Services / 93
- Managing Reference Services / 95
- Measuring and Evaluating the Use of Archives / 97

Chapter 9   **The Future of Reference Services In Archives** / 105

Bibliographical Essay / 109

Appendices / 114

Preface

The seven new titles in SAA's Archival Fundamentals Series have been conceived and written to be a foundation for modern archival theory and practice. Like the previous Basic Manual Series that for more than a dozen years excelled in articulating and advancing archival knowledge and skills, they too are intended for a *general* audience within the archival profession and to have widespread application. They will strengthen and augment the knowledge and skills of archivists, general practitioners and specialists alike, who are performing a wide range of archival duties in all types of archival and manuscript repositories.

This series is designed to encompass the basic archival functions enumerated by SAA's Guidelines for Graduate Archival Education. The volumes discuss the theoretical principles that underlie archival practice, the functions and activities that are common within the archival profession, and the techniques that represent the best of current practice. They give practical advice, enabling today's practitioners to prepare for the challenges of rapid change within the archival profession.

Together with more specialized manuals also available from SAA, the Archival Fundamentals Series should form the core of any archivist's working library. The series has particular value for newcomers to the profession, including students, who wish to have a broad overview of archival work and an in-depth treatment of its major components. The volumes in the series will also serve as invaluable guides and reference works for more experienced archivists, especially in working with new staff members, volunteers, and others. It is our hope that the Archival Fundamentals Series will be a benchmark in the archival literature for many years to come.

Preparing this series and volume has been a collaborative effort. SAA readers, reviewers, staff members, and Editorial Board members have assisted greatly. We would particularly like to thank Donn Neal, Tim Ericson, and Anne Diffendal, executive directors; Susan Grigg, Chair of the Editorial Board, whose good counsel and support never failed; Roger Fromm, Photographic Editor; and Teresa Brinati, Managing Editor, who brought the volumes from text to publication.

In addition, the Society expresses its deep appreciation to the National Historical Publications and Records Commission, which funded the preparation and initial printing of the series.

Mary Jo Pugh
Archival Fundamentals Series Editor

Julia Marks Young
Volume Editor

Acknowledgements

While editing the other volumes in this series and writing this one, I discovered anew the ease of exhorting others to do well and the difficulty of doing so myself. I have relied so heavily upon the advice and assistance of so many people in writing this volume that I have at times felt like the Chair of the Ad Hoc Committee on the Reference Manual. I cannot adequately express my gratitude to Nancy Bartlett, Kathleen Marquis, Paul Conway, Rand Jimerson, Tim Ericson, Suzanne Flandreau, Trudy Peterson, and the two anonymous but helpful reviewers of the manual. Every sentence should be footnoted. Roger Fromm and Teresa Brinati made the volume real. Susan Grigg, chair of the Editorial Board, was consistently patient, encouraging, and helpful. All these good people saved me from much foolishness but cannot be held responsible for errors or omissions that remain.

My editor, Julia Young, was rigorous, thoughtful, thorough, and kind. It is not often that you find someone who is a good friend and a good writer.

As always, I relied on Thomas Michael McCort. My children Katie and Christopher were remarkably patient with this sibling who took so much of their time.

Mary Jo Pugh

A Sonnet to Archivy

As barren fields in wintertime are lined
With broken stalks and ears of corn long spent,
So records are the stubble of mankind—
They have no life, and give no nourishment.
They are the words and numbers of the past,
The dry, misshapen kernels in the bran,
Like chaff stripped from the germ, they cannot last—
Yet you do make them feed the mind of Man.
Then hearty, golden grains these records be:
They are the endless grist of History.

Thomas Michael McCort
1982

Chapter 1

Reference Services in Archives

Archival and manuscript repositories identify and preserve records of enduring value; most importantly, they make them available for use. Reference services in archival and manuscript repositories assist users, and potential users, in using archival holdings and locating information they need. Archives are tools; like all tools, they are kept to be used.

Origin and Diversity of Archives

Archives are the records of organizations, created or accumulated in the course of daily activities, and saved by the creator because they may be useful for continuing administration or for later research. Although archives are retained by the organization that created them, they may have as much or more value for researchers outside the organization, as part of the cultural heritage linking past and present.

Historical manuscripts are the papers of individuals. Like archives, they are records generated in the course of daily activities. They are collected by manuscript repositories because of their research value. Manuscript repositories also collect the records of organizations that do not maintain their own archives.

Today, the word "archives" is often used to refer both to organizational records and historical manuscripts. That is, archives are all records of enduring value created in the course of daily activity, whether organizational or personal. In this manual, archives will generally be used in this broader sense, except in those cases in which there are significant differences in the use of organizational archives and

historical manuscripts. To further complicate matters, the English language also uses the word "archives" to refer both to the building that houses records of enduring value and to the agency charged with responsibility for identifying, preserving, and using them. The reader must be alert to context to ascertain the meaning intended.

Archival agencies differ from libraries in the materials they hold. Libraries collect written accounts consciously created and widely disseminated to inform, educate, entertain, or enrich a general audience. Individual items are self-contained and self-explanatory. In contrast, archives preserve documentary expressions created to communicate to a defined audience, often a particular individual, for a specific purpose. Archival documents result from the activity they record, and can be understood only in the context of other documents created by the same activity over time. These unique aggregations of records, created as the by-product of daily activity, are saved for future use, both by their creators and by later researchers.

Thus, it is not the form of materials, whether published or unpublished, that distinguishes libraries and archives, as many assume. Rather the difference stems from the purpose for which the documents are created.[1] Archival materials consist of a wide variety of forms, many requiring special conditions of use. They typically comprise correspondence, diaries, case files, memoranda, circulars, and

[1] Frank Burke, "Similarities and Differences" in *Archive-Library Relations* (New York: R. R. Bowker Company, 1976), 31-35.

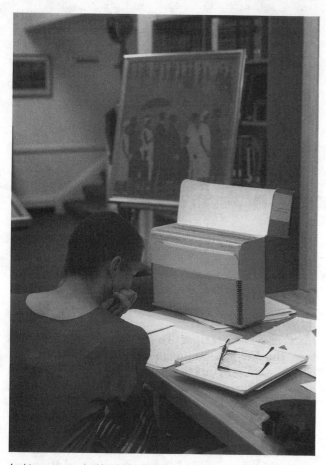

Archives are tools; like all tools, they are kept to be used. (*Andrew Simons, courtesy of Amistad Research Center, Tulane University*)

such as businesses, churches, voluntary associations, universities, and museums, establish institutional archives to care for their records. Such private archives are likely to be kept primarily to meet long-term administrative, legal, or fiscal needs of the institution itself. When such an organization keeps its records because of their continuing usefulness for its ongoing business, *administrative use* is the primary rationale, and reference services are provided mainly to the creators of the records and their successors.

Research by users outside the originating organization is another rationale for keeping archives and the primary rationale for preserving historical manuscripts. Since manuscript repositories collect the papers of individuals and the records of outside organizations so that they can be used for historical research, providing reference services to researchers will have a higher priority in this type of repository than providing administrative reference services to the creators of the records.

Governmental archives have an additional responsibility for *public use,* to protect the rights of the people. Public archives preserve records of individual rights and benefits. As a "cornerstone of democracy," public archives also provide for government accountability by preserving records that enable citizens to monitor the conduct of the people's business and the performance of official servants. Reference services in public archives serve all citizens.[3]

While the mission of the parent institution guides priorities for reference services, the cultural value of archives as the memory of civilization transcends the current uses of records in the organizations that create or preserve them. When considering the needs of users, archivists must balance these enduring cultural values against the immediate practical needs of the organizations that pay to preserve records. These short-term and long-term values may conflict as archivists provide access and reference services for the primary user groups—as identified by the mission of the parent institution—and also seek to meet the cultural needs of the larger society.

other unpublished textual records. They may also, however, contain documents published in the course of organizational activity, such as reports, directories, posters, or advertisements. Modern archives also include photographs, films, sound recordings, and, increasingly, electronic records.

Although their holdings differ, libraries and archives share many common activities and a common mission. Both select, preserve, organize, and make available information in documentary form. Both libraries and archives are institutions whose mission is to preserve our collective memory, to make accumulated knowledge available for present and future use.[2]

Rationales for Archives

The use of archives depends, in part, on the mission of the repository. Many corporate entities,

Historical Developments in the Use of Archives

Reference services and access policies in an archival or manuscript repository can be best understood by knowing the repository's history and appre-

---

[2] This theme is developed in *Archives and Library Administration: Divergent Traditions and Common Concerns* (New York: Haworth, 1986). See especially David Klaassen, "The Provenance of Archives Under Library Administration," 37.

[3] Don Wilson, Archivist of the United States, referred to archives as the cornerstone of democracy.

ciating its relationship to the historical development of archives. Early archives were primarily the records of governments, and until the French Revolution, governmental archives were used primarily by sovereigns and their servants. The archives of private institutions such as universities and churches also were generally used only by their administrators.

During the French Revolution, public use of governmental archives was recognized. The new French government declared that its archives were the property of the people, the source of sovereignty in a democratic society, and accessible to the people. Other Western nations also adopted the concept of public access to public records. In the United States, this principle, often called the *public archives tradition,* was enunciated from the beginning of settlement, although governmental archives were slow to develop. Interest in public archives gained momentum only at the end of the nineteenth century with the development of an identifiable historical profession and with reformers' interest in better management of governmental activities. The first true state archives was founded in Alabama in 1901; the National Archives was founded in 1934.[4]

Modern manuscript repositories are descendants of the libraries of medieval monasteries and universities, which, before the invention of the printing press, copied and collected literary and scholarly texts for research. In the nineteenth century, university libraries, manuscript libraries, and historical societies also began to collect unpublished records created in the course of private activity, such as personal and family letters, diaries, drafts of literary productions, notes, and the like. Manuscript libraries, administered by scholars for the use of scholars, usually provided access only to researchers with academic affiliations. The narrow elitism of this research-based *historical manuscripts tradition* persisted well into the twentieth century. Howard Peckham stated in 1956 that the research library is not a public library. "If it should open its doors to competent scholars, then it should close them to those who are not competent."[5]

In the United States, collecting and preserving historical records centered at first in private historical societies. These were composed of gentleman scholars who collected the manuscripts of the great men and great families of the Eastern seaboard. In the mid-nineteenth century, publicly-funded historical societies in the Middle West began to collect the manuscripts and reminiscences of early settlers and pioneer families. In addition to collecting papers of prominent individuals and families for historical and genealogical research, historical societies also edited and published significant manuscripts.

These differing institutional purposes and histories gave rise to a sometimes confusing welter of institutional policies for access to archival materials, and divergent views of the appropriate and permissible uses of archives and manuscripts. Private archives and scholarly research libraries tended to limit access, in the first case to administrators of the creating institution and in the second to recognized scholars. In contrast, most governmental archives and publicly-funded historical societies opened access more broadly.

Since the 1960s the trend has been to open access to a broader public. Freedom of information legislation, open meeting requirements, and sunshine laws provided wider access to information in the public sphere generally, and this sense of the public's right to know spilled over to archives as well. The predominance of the public archives tradition, the development of national guides and national standards, and the standardizing tendencies of funding agencies like the National Historical Publications and Records Commission and the National Endowment for the Humanities have strengthened the trend to wider access. The Society of American Archivists has also taken an important role in melding these divergent institutional traditions into a professional whole and in setting professional models for reference services, access policies, professional ethics, and outreach activities.

Consequently, the archival profession has moved from a custodial role, in which the archivist's primary duty was to protect repository collections by limiting use, to a more activist role promoting the wider use of archives. The change in professional culture has caused occasional conflict between traditional practice and new attitudes. Today, most archivists emphasize service to a broad public and seek to develop new constituencies to support archival programs. Archivists' attention to reference services and user education reflects a desire both to enlarge constituencies and to respond to their needs.

---

[4] The development of these traditions in the United States is described in Richard Berner, *Archival Theory and Practice in the United States: A Historical Analysis* (Seattle: University of Washington Press, 1983).

[5] Howard Peckham, "Aiding the Scholar in Using Manuscript Collections," *American Archivist* 19 (July 1956): 221-28.

Access to Archives

To use archives, users need intellectual, legal, and physical access to them. In the broadest sense, access refers to the process of identifying and locating records likely to contain information useful for solving problems. Access in this sense is *intellectual* access, provided both through the arrangement and description of records and through reference assistance. Archivists arrange records according to basic tenets of provenance and original order, to retain evidence of the activities that created them. That is, records from different sources are not intermingled, and the original filing order of the creator, if usable, is retained. Such principles of arrangement insure both that records will continue to be useful for the creating organization and that later users can evaluate the content of records in the context of their creation. Repositories use a wide variety of reference tools, known as finding aids, to describe their holdings and provide reference assistance to help users locate needed records and information.

In a narrower, *legal*, sense, access can mean the authority or permission to use archives. Records created initially for personal or internal use may contain private or confidential information that should not be disseminated immediately. Problems of privacy and confidentiality can arise when records created for limited circulation to carry out specific activities are made available to the public. Use of archives may thus be conditioned by legal and ethical issues: most importantly, privacy, confidentiality, freedom of information, and copyright. Archivists strive to provide fair, equitable access to records in their care, but they must also protect information affecting creators or third parties until it is no longer sensitive.

Access may also mean *physical* access, the opportunity to examine documents. Repositories provide physical access by maintaining regular and sufficient hours of operation, providing space to study records, and enabling users to copy information from records. While meeting these needs of current researchers, archivists must also consider those of future users by protecting archives from theft or abuse and from wear and tear.

Reference Services in Archives

Reference services, broadly conceived, are the activities by which archivists bring users and records

Figure 1-1   Reference Services in Archives

Reference services in archives provide:
- ▼ Information about the repository
- ▼ Information about holdings
- ▼ Information from holdings
- ▼ Information about records creators
- ▼ Referrals to other repositories or resources
- ▼ Information about copyright, privacy, confidentiality, freedom of information, and other relevant laws
- ▼ Instruction in using archives and the research process
- ▼ Physical access to holdings
- ▼ Copies of holdings
- ▼ Loans from holdings

together to meet user needs. As listed in Figure 1-1, they encompass a wide variety of activities and call upon intellectual, administrative, and interpersonal skills. Reference services can take place in the research room, by telephone or mail, or by electronic mail systems or fax. Reference services are also provided through public programs both inside and outside the repository. In a small repository, such intellectual, administrative, and interpersonal activities may be the responsibility of one person; in a large repository, they may be shared by several professional staff members as well as paraprofessional and clerical staff.

Intellectual Components of Reference Services. Facilitating research, undertaking research, and educating users are three important intellectual components of reference service in archives. To facilitate research, reference archivists help users find records that meet their information needs. Reference inquiries may be initiated by mail, fax, electronic mail, and telephone as well as in person. Users bring a wide variety of research needs to archives, and archivists help them refine their questions and organize search strategies. Although finding aids are increasingly standardized, most repositories have accumulated a wide variety of finding aids that may not yet be integrated into a repository-wide system. Such diversity of finding aids often requires the mediation of archivists before users can understand them. Most users also need information about repository rules and procedures and information about legal and physical access to archival materials.

Once likely records are identified, researchers often request assistance in using them. Because ar-

Archivist and researcher are partners in research. (*Greg Koep, courtesy of New Jersey Historical Society*)

chives are the products of activities, understanding them requires knowledge of the organizations and individuals that created them. Archivists and users must understand the historical conditions, organizational communications patterns, and technical processes that produced the records in order to evaluate the information they contain. Archival arrangement according to provenance, though necessary to understanding organizational context, is unfamiliar to many users and may present some initial difficulties for users outside the organization or even for later users from the organization.

Facilitating research requires continuing interaction between archivist and user throughout the research project. This may not be completed until the last question regarding copyright and citation is answered. In addition to using records and descriptive tools within the repository, reference archivists often facilitate research by referring researchers to other sources beyond the repository.

Undertaking research is a second important intellectual role. Reference archivists undertake research themselves to learn about the parent organization and history of records creators, to understand the functions and forms of records, to place the finding aids and records in context, to locate information in the records for others who cannot do so themselves, and to interpret records or information for users.

Promoting appreciation and use of records may involve locating, synthesizing, and disseminating archival information through exhibitions, publications, speeches, and other educational programs. Such public programs seek to make historical information accessible to the public. Archivists use holdings to write books and articles, develop exhibits, produce slide-tape shows, and create film documentaries. In these products they select and analyze historical information, tell a story, and inform a wider public of the content of records. In short, archivists are users themselves and present their products to the public as other users do, with the goal of informing, educating, or entertaining the public. Learning about a historical event or issue may stimulate potential users who have not thought of using archival sources because they do not know of them or have not related their question to archival sources. "Public programs publicize the products of research and the availability of the information in records, encouraging a variety of users who are not reached through traditional means."[6]

Educating individual users in the research room and groups through public programs is a third significant intellectual function of the reference archivist. Few users have experience with primary sources, and most are unprepared for the complexity of archival sources, finding aids, and archival practice. Most have no experience integrating and understanding the undigested mass of information so often found in primary sources. Although every schoolchild is taught how to use library classification and catalogs, many archival users have never encountered archival arrangement and archival finding aids. Many users need instruction to understand primary sources and the finding aids that describe them.

Educating users to make better use of archives is an essential part of reference work. Beyond daily teaching in the research room, many archivists find

⁶ Elsie Freeman, "Public Programs: What Alice Didn't Say," *SAA Reference, Access, and Outreach Newsletter* 2 (August 1987): 3-4, and "Educational Programs as Administrative Function," *American Archivist* 41 (April 1978): 147-53.

education in a broader sense part of their institutional mission. Since reference archivists encourage the use of records, educational programs grow naturally from reference functions. Public programs such as orientation sessions, workshops, handouts, or introductory slide-tape or video presentations extend the ability of the reference archivist to help users to be more efficient in exploiting archives.

Interpersonal Components of Reference Services. Because archival reference service is frequently very personalized, good communication between users and archivists is critical. Research indicates that more than half of the information exchanged between two people is expressed nonverbally by gestures, tone, and attitude.[7] Verbal and nonverbal communications must be congruent.

Archivists and users may have very different expectations about the reference interaction. Discrepancies in expectations may cause confusion, disappointment, or failure to use archival holdings effectively. For example, users and archivists may differ in their expectations of the conditions under which archival materials are to be used. In some repositories users must apply in advance for admission. Expecting archives to be like libraries, users may feel rebuffed if they cannot be accommodated without an appointment. Because archives must ensure the integrity of unique materials, most require users to submit to rigorous security provisions; users who prefer to be left alone may find archival registration and security procedures intrusive or annoying. Archivists must remember that if they are not careful, the first message they give to users is, "We think you are a thief," or "We think you are not worthy to use these materials."

Users and archivists may also have different expectations about the appropriate role of the archivist and the amount of time required to locate needed information. Most archivists expect to provide instruction in using finding aids and guidance to records likely to contain needed information, but many users expect archivists to furnish information directly. Usually archivists have neither the time nor resources to do so.

Policies and priorities must be clearly and convincingly communicated; they must also be reviewed regularly to recognize changing publics and user needs. Although users come from many disciplines and backgrounds, most repositories were established to serve either administrators of the parent institution or scholars. Inherited finding aids, architectural barriers, and procedures that work well for experienced users may need to be revised to meet the needs of current users.

Archivists should strive to make every user feel welcome and to treat all users fairly. Research in archives requires an effective partnership between archivists and users. Sensitivity, clarity, and a genuine spirit of public service are needed to ensure successful interpersonal relationships in archival reference services.

Administrative Components of Reference Services. Administering the daily tasks of reference services, or managing the staff providing them, may be the most time-consuming aspect of archival reference services. Among the many administrative tasks required for the smooth operation of reference services are receiving, identifying, orienting, and registering users; locating and paging materials; and supervising copying and loans. Administering reference services often appears to create "forms, forms, and more forms," but the administrative role goes beyond this daily routine.[8]

The daily practice of reference services must be grounded in administrative policy. Identifying appropriate policies and efficient procedures and ensuring fair and equitable treatment for all users are important managerial tasks for reference archivists. Further, reference archivists must advocate user needs in repository planning and relay user information to other repository staff.

Reference archivists stand at the intersection of users, finding aids, repository staff, and records. In essence, they direct traffic through the intersection. They must balance and integrate the intellectual, interpersonal, and administrative elements of reference services to meet the needs of users, protect records, and promote the most effective use of repository resources.

Ethics of Reference Services

Because the success of reference service turns on negotiating a series of balances, its ethical dimensions assume considerable importance. Archivists respond to inquiries and promote the use of their holdings. While making records available for use as widely as possible, archivists must protect the legiti-

---

[7] Joanna Lopez Muñoz, "The Significance of NonVerbal Communications in the Reference Interview," *RQ* 16 (Spring 1977): 220.

[8] Kathleen Marquis referred to the "forms, forms, forms" nature of archival reference service. I am indebted to Nancy Bartlett for stimulating me to think about the management of archival reference services.

mate needs of the creators of records and the privacy rights of third parties identified in them. Even when information from holdings cannot be supplied, repositories are obliged to provide information about themselves and their holdings. Archivists strive to supply all documents of interest to a researcher, although meeting this obligation may be difficult, given the arrangement and descriptive practices of most repositories. Reference archivists must respect the confidentiality of the reference interview and divulge the details of users' research only with permission. Careful formulation of policies and training of staff are needed to ensure fair and equitable access and service for all researchers.[9]

Promoting the Use of Archives

Outreach and advocacy touch many aspects of archival management—funding, donor relations, acquisitions, and use—and their treatment in a manual devoted to reference services must necessarily be limited. Reference archivists are, however, well situated to encourage the wider use of archives and to educate users and potential users about the value and use of archives.

Archivists sometimes have reservations about promoting the wider use of their repositories because of limited physical facilities and staff resources. Although greater numbers of users may increase the workload for the staff, the repository can use the demands of increased numbers to argue for greater support from resource allocators. Without strong constituencies to advocate increased resources, it is likely that funding for archives will remain low.

Users can also be resources for the repository. Users, like records creators, may help identify records of enduring value and work to preserve them. Many users volunteer for such time-consuming but significant tasks as preparing materials for microfilming or indexing records. Users can also contribute significantly to outreach activities that make archival resources better known.

Promotion of archives is closely tied to the future of reference services. Unless archivists develop varied and vocal constituencies today, it is unlikely that archival repositories will have the resources necessary to identify, preserve, and make available the cultural resources needed in the future. Identifying the products and services that archives provide to their parent institution and to other user constituencies, thinking creatively about the costs and venues for providing them, and publicizing them aggressively are necessary to sustain the archival mission in the developing information economy.

Goals of this Manual

This manual will describe policies and procedures for reference services that represent a commonly accepted professional standard. It will deal primarily with providing intellectual, legal, and physical access to textual records, with only limited attention to other record forms. In administering reference services, policy must come first; procedures should reflect established policies. Any reference program must be flexible enough to accommodate itself to the unique characteristics of its particular archives. Each repository will need to adapt these general policies and procedures to its own conditions and codify them in a repository procedures manual.

What cannot be codified either in this manual or in a repository manual is the joy of reference work. It can bring great personal satisfaction. The excitement of the hunt for information is followed by the satisfaction of the find. Reference archivists feel personal accomplishment in locating information or records that could not be found without their knowledge and skills. Reference archivists satisfy their own curiosity about historical events as they assist others. They apply their historical knowledge and build their own research skills. The amazing variety of questions from users stimulates intellectual growth; answering one question raises yet new questions. The serendipity of research, the unexpected discovery of new sources and insights, frequently entertains and delights.

---

[9] "A Code of Ethics for Archivists," *American Archivist* 43 (Summer 1980): 415-18; *SAA Newsletter,* July 1991.

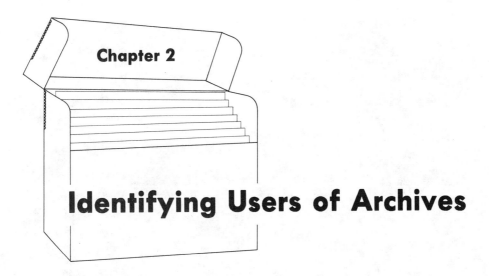

Chapter 2

Identifying Users of Archives

Many people use archives, both directly and indirectly, and others could benefit from using them. People use them because the information found in archives is useful outside the repository. Archives can be put to a variety of uses and result in a variety of products. In providing reference services, reference archivists must understand each user's particular information need. Individual users can be analyzed in terms of their research purpose, intended uses of archival information, types of questions asked, and degree of experience and preparation. In planning reference programs to meet current research needs and in designing outreach programs for potential users, repositories need to identify specific communities of users and their needs.

The Values of Archives

In the research room of any archival repository one can find people searching finding aids, identifying records, and requesting, reading, copying, and citing them. These activities can be measured quantitatively, and as we will see in Chapter 8, archivists frequently compile such numbers to report the use of archives. It is more important, however, to ascertain *why* people use records.

Organizations and individuals create records initially to carry out administrative, fiscal, economic, social, legal, or other activities. These are the primary values of the records. Some records, those transferred to archives, also have secondary value for later researchers.

Secondary values include informational value, evidential value, and intrinsic value. *Informational*

value is the most straightforward. It describes the facts that records contain about people, events, objects, or places. In the course of daily activities, records creators record information about the objects of their activities or the places in which they occur. For example, a report may provide information about the number of new accounts opened.

Evidential value refers to the information (or evidence) that records provide about their creators or the activities that generated them. Information in archives gains much of its value from its context, which reflects patterns of action and documents accountability. For example, that a report is in the files of the recipient indicates that the report was sent and received; a carbon copy of the response to it in the same file indicates that it was read. Thus file contents and filing structures can be as important for documenting the flow of information as for retrieving the information itself.

Intrinsic value describes the value that records have as artifacts—as symbols, or tangible links to the past. The Declaration of Independence has been reproduced many times, but the original document still awes citizens viewing it in the National Archives. One of the twenty-three known examples of the first printed Declaration sold for $1.5 million; what price could be put on the handwritten original document?[1] Similarly, families treasure family photographs or a Bible with handwritten entries of baptisms, marriages, and burials of their ancestors, for these are tangible links to their past.

---

[1] "Declaration Breaks Records," *San Francisco Chronicle Review,* 4 March 1990, 15.

In a busy research room users locate, request, and study documents. (*Balch Institute for Ethnic Studies, Philadelphia*)

Uses of Archives

Use of archives may be direct or indirect. *Direct use* occurs when someone obtains information from a record or draws on a record as evidence of the activity that it documents. In these instances, users are people "with a need or wish to know information found in records of enduring value."[2] Also called researchers, patrons, or clients, such users initiate contact with the repository directly, either in person, by phone, or by mail. Direct use can be measured when someone reads a document in the repository, obtains a copy by mail, or receives information by telephone or letter. Loaning documents is another type of direct use.

Direct users also include anyone "who for any reason needs the services of an archivist or an archives."[3] For example, archivists may supply administrators with information about the organization's history taken from archival holdings or from administrative histories compiled to manage records. Records creators also use archival services when an archivist determines the disposition of a series of records. Likewise, archivists may assist individuals wishing to preserve family papers.

Identifying *indirect use* is more difficult. Indirect users are "the potential beneficiaries of the historical information found in archives."[4] Indirect users may never enter an archives, but benefit

[2] *An Action Agenda for the Archival Profession: Institutionalizing the Planning Process* (Chicago: Society of American Archivists, 1988), 66.

[3] *Action Agenda*, 66.
[4] *Action Agenda*, 66; also Paul Conway, "Facts and Frameworks: An Approach to Studying the Users of Archives," *American Archivist* 49 (Fall 1986): 396.

nevertheless from archival information by using the many and varied products of the direct use of historical information. Though a small number of researchers actually use archives, their work has a "multiplier effect," transmitting information that affects how others think about themselves and their past.[5] Books, newspaper and periodical articles, dissertations and theses, genealogies, speeches, term papers, films, television documentaries, slide shows, exhibits, legal briefs, environmental impact statements, and other policy documents are some of the products that convey information and evidence derived from archival holdings.

Identifying Individual Needs

Most people come to archival repositories because they need to solve problems that require historical information or evidence found in archival holdings, not because they want to use historical records as such. Although some users find the age, rarity, or beauty of original documents as important as the information or evidence they contain, people generally seek solutions to their information problems, not particular objects. To borrow Elsie Freeman's apt illustration, although people go to the hardware store to buy quarter-inch drill bits, they are really buying quarter-inch holes, and if there is a better way to get the desired results, they will no longer buy quarter-inch bits.[6] So it is with archives: if archival repositories do not meet the information needs of users, users will not come to archives.

Many people who could benefit from information available in archives do not use archives because they do not know that archives have the kinds of information they seek. Others do not use archives because they think using archives is too time consuming or too daunting. Some may think that archives are not open to them. As we will see in Chapter 8, archivists can conduct research to discover the information needs and attitudes of potential users and design reference and public programs to meet them.

Reference archivists need to understand who is consulting what types of information for what purposes. The needs of direct users differ depending on their research purpose, the uses they intend to make of archival information, the type of information

sought, the types of questions they ask, and their experience and preparation.

Research purpose is in part determined by whether the user's information problem is motivated by work requirements or by personal interest. Most people come to archives because their work, often on behalf of a company, government, association, university, or client, requires it. Other researchers come to archives because they want to, seeking information for enjoyment, recreation, or private use.

The user's occupation or discipline has a large impact on the information requested and research methodologies employed. On a practical level, a user's occupation affects time available for research. Those whose work requires archival research find business hours satisfactory. Many of those seeking information for enjoyment, recreation, or private use find business hours, or abbreviated weekend and evening hours very limiting, though business hours may be satisfactory for retired individuals who have finally gained the time to devote to research.

The intended use of information—report, film, exhibit, family history, book, article, legal brief, advertisement, or environmental impact statement—affects the types of information sought and the questions asked. It is helpful to distinguish between the form or genre of information and the media on which it is stored. Reference archivists need to understand the form of evidence that researchers require for their intended use. For example, congressional hearings may be stored on various media such as paper transcripts, sound recordings, or video recordings.

Some information needs are "applicational," such as the need for a specific document to provide evidence to solve a particular problem or to illustrate a point. An exploratory study of reference queries found that 56 percent of all questions about holdings sought specific items.[7] Other information needs are "abstract," to increase general understanding or competence. Thus, users typically bring two types of questions to archives: factual and interpretive. Researchers with factual questions approach archives with closed-ended questions, seeking a particular document, or seeking specific information about a particular person, place, object, or event. Their questions are precise and focused, asking, "Who, What, Where, When, How many, or How much?" In contrast, researchers with interpretive questions read comprehensively through a body of material to

---

[5] Page Putnam Miller, *Developing a Premier National Institution: A Report from the User Community to the National Archives* (Washington: National Coordinating Committee for the Promotion of History, 1989), 9.

[6] Elsie Freeman, "Buying Quarter Inch Holes: Public Support through Results," *Midwestern Archivist* 10 (1985): 89-97.

[7] Colin Mick, "Human Factors in Information Work," *ASIS* 17 (1980): 21-23; David Bearman, "User Presentation Language in Archives," *Archives and Museum Informatics* 3 (Winter 1989-90): 3-7.

tell a story, develop a narrative, or test a hypothesis. Posing open-ended questions, they seek to answer broad questions of motivation, causality, and change. They ask the question, "Why?"[8]

Degree of experience in archival research is another variable affecting user needs. Many users, regardless of discipline or nature of inquiry, are not well-versed in archival research and need help in conceptualizing the research process. They need help from archivists to analyze the process of finding relevant documentation and devising search strategies. Once novices are launched on their research, they may need assistance deciphering handwriting, understanding dating conventions and abbreviations, or interpreting slang and references to contemporary events. Many ready reference questions can be answered with such standard bibliographical tools as the *Dictionary of American Biography,* the *Encyclopedia of American History,* and local reference sources; the archivist may have to teach newcomers to use these sources. Although archivists may imagine that it is particularly urgent to teach young or novice users proper care of manuscripts and photographs, they often find that new users, more in awe of original sources than experienced users, treat materials with more respect.

It is difficult to predict how much staff time is required to assist users. In general, the less experienced the researcher the more important the educational role of the reference archivist in providing intellectual access. In some cases, however, because more experienced researchers bring more complex reference requests, they require greater assistance from the reference archivist. Since they are more efficient at using larger quantities of material, more experienced researchers may also require more time from support staff for retrieving materials and photocopying.

The degree of preparation for any particular project or visit also affects reference requirements. One archivist suggests that historians may go through three stages in the course of their research. First, a historian may canvass large bodies of material to define the scope of a research problem and the sources available. Second, after defining a topic, the historian may use particular bodies of records intensively. Finally, after writing has begun, the his-

torian may seek to verify particular points and ask very specific questions.[9]

Identifying Services and Programs for User Groups

Thus the needs of individual users can be analyzed in terms of their research purpose, intended uses of information, types of questions asked, and degree of experience. Planning for reference services, however, often requires identifying programs to meet the needs of particular communities of users. Although systematic research into the nature of archival constituencies has just begun, experience suggests that most users can be grouped into seven constituencies, primarily on the basis of research purpose. Significant vocational groups are the staff of the creating institution (including archivists), professional users, academic scholars, students, and teachers. Primary avocational users are genealogists and avocational historians.

It is important to note that a given individual might fit in one category one day and another on another day. For example, a member of the staff of the creating institution might also be enrolled as a university student or engaged in genealogical research. For purposes of repository planning, a student working for the parent institution during a summer internship is a staff member, not a student. Understanding who visits an archives is essentially a matter of identifying each person's group affiliation as it relates to the reason they visit. Asking for a person's occupation or institutional affiliation is necessary only if relevant to understanding the information problem. Ultimately, reference archivists must treat each user as an individual, worthy of respect and attention, regardless of occupation, type of research, or experience.

Vocational Users.

1. Staff of the Parent Institution. Staff of the parent institution are an important user population. Archives, the corporate memory of the institution, are preserved so that the parent institution can understand its history and the sources of current policy, and maximize its return on its information resources. Archives are used to ensure continuity, build on experience, and identify solutions for current problems. Use of archives can help prevent repetition of failed solutions for recurring problems.

---

[8] William L. Joyce formulates a similar distinction in "Archivists and Research Use," *American Archivist* 47 (Spring 1984): 124-33. Trudy Peterson and Nancy Bartlett shared unpublished works that explore this distinction.

[9] Lawrence Dowler, "The Role of Use in Defining Archival Principle and Practice: A Research Agenda for the Availability and Use of Records," *American Archivist* 51 (Winter and Spring 1988): 79.

Staff use records to document the infrastructure of the organization, be it the buildings that house it, or, in the case of governmental records, the very fabric of public life, such as roads and bridges. Maintenance, repair, and public safety depend on good records. Legal staff seek precedents, the terms of gifts, or evidence for current litigation.

Staff members turn to the archives to prepare for celebrations of notable events because archival records document the founding, purposes, and development of the institution. Marketing, public relations, and personnel staff may seek illustrations and other visual materials for advertisements, commercials, training films, employee information brochures, publications, exhibitions, videos, films, and slide shows to help explain the organization to employees and the public. They request apt and colorful quotations for speeches and publications. Staff in some corporations use archives for customer service research, and development staff in membership organizations find archival information useful for fund-raising.

Many staff questions are factual, not interpretive. Staff members often seek an illustration, quota-

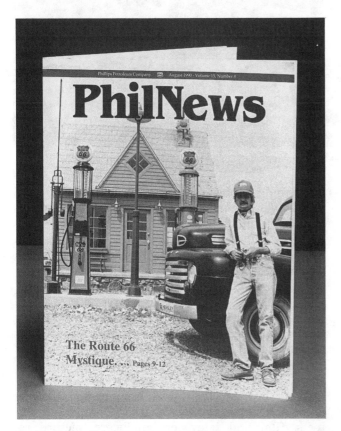

A corporate staff magazine features historical photographs. (*Greg Booker, courtesy of Phillips Petroleum Company*)

tion, or verification of a "first." Staff often request a known document in the records of a particular unit, but seemingly simple requests may require considerable reference time if the exact date and circumstances of creation of the document are imprecise or if the existence of the document is confirmed only by memory or by brief subsequent references.

Since administrators of the parent institution are simultaneously creators and users of archives, access and reference policies may give priority to their requests. Prompt and appropriate response justifies the archives to its resource allocators. For administrative archives, especially those newly established, a successful program requires a wide range of reference services to the parent. "Through a continued effort to establish an image of usefulness through its reference services, the archives can establish its validity and role in the organization of which it is a part."[10] Manuscript repositories need similar policies for determining levels of service for donors of personal papers and for organizations that deposit their records.

Archives can fulfill their roles in the parent organization only if administrators are aware of the resources of the archives and know how to use them. Archivists have many tools to educate staff about the archives. They may send brochures and copies of finding aids to new employees. Inviting department heads, secretaries, and administrative assistants to visit the archives and to discuss information needs can build effective relationships. Archivists can use organization newsletters, publications, and exhibitions to inform employees of archival holdings. Celebrations such as anniversaries are opportunities to demonstrate the resources and services of the archives, and because of their knowledge of organizational history, archivists can be key contributors to such events.

An archives can become indispensable to its parent organization if it serves as a broker for information about institutional history, functions, internal operations, and activities—that is, if it truly acts as a corporate memory, not simply storing such information but making it known. The archives itself uses such information to identify, organize, and describe organizational records; if promoted aggressively, this information may become the basis for

---

[10] Thomas Wilsted, "Establishing an Image: The Role of Reference Service in a New Archival Program," *Reference Services in Archives* (New York: Haworth Press, 1986), 171.

An archivist leads an orientation seminar for staff members of the parent organization. (*Association of American Medical Colleges*)

making the archives the center of the organization's information system.[11]

Archivists themselves may be among the most important users of their own archives, particularly as intermediaries for other users, both from within the parent institution and from outside it. Responding to telephone and mail inquiries is an important part of reference service in most repositories. Archivists frequently interpret the inventories, catalogs, and other finding aids, or use them to look for information for records creators or other users. Archivists locate specific information or documents for factual researchers and assist interpretive research-

ers in finding relevant sources. As institutional staff themselves, archivists are most likely to be knowledgeable about its history and organization. They can draw the attention of the institution to relevant precedents, policies, and documents. Archivists disseminate information from the archives through letters, phone calls, copies, publications, exhibitions, and educational programs.

2. Professional Users. In much the same way that staff members use archives on behalf of the parent institution, others also use archival resources in their work. These users, here called professional users, for lack of a better term, represent many professions: lawyers, legislators, engineers, landscape architects, preservationists, urban planners, architects, film and television producers, picture researchers, journalists, and publishers. Although they may not be trained as historians, they ask his-

---

[11] David Bearman, among others, has argued for this perspective. See *Archival Methods* (Pittsburgh: Archives and Museums Informatics, 1989), 44; and Bearman and Richard H. Lytle, "The Power of the Principle of Provenance," *Archivaria* 21 (1985): 14-27.

torical questions and use archival sources to answer them.[12]

These professionals are direct users linking archival sources to many indirect users, since many of their professions use archival information on behalf of groups, clients, firms, governments, or professional associations. Examples of the dramatic impact of historical information on current policies abound. Environmental impact statements identify toxic waste sites threatening municipal water supplies. Civil rights suits document past discrimination and gain monetary awards or affirmative action plans. Archaeological impact statements alter building plans. Geneticists trace the genealogical component of many diseases. Historical preservation documentation qualifies structures for tax credits and encourages the adaptive reuse of old buildings. Indian tribes win large settlements by establishing the true value of lands ceded for token payments in the nineteenth century. Mining companies use historical records to locate former mines and tailings for reworking. Historical accounts are used to locate and map the activity of earthquake faults. And in the West, vital water rights depend on historical allocations.

Films, especially television documentaries, are one of the most important means by which historical information is used by the public. Approximately seven million viewers have seen each of the historical films in the Public Broadcasting Service series *The American Experience,* and millions more see classroom rebroadcasts. Some fourteen million people watched *The Civil War* in October 1990, and thousands requested copies of the moving letter written by Major Sullivan Ballou to his wife Sarah from the Illinois State Historical Library. Documentaries using historical materials explore such topics as prohibition, the civil rights movement, or the internment of Japanese-Americans during World War II. These programs shape present-day conceptions by deepening understanding of the past. Photographs used in publications, posters, and advertisements are another important means by which historical information is transmitted to the public.[13]

As part of its decor, a restaurant displays historical photogrtaphs of a local college. (*Harry's Grille, Magee Enterprises, Bloomsburg, Pennsylvania*)

Professionals using archives may expect considerable reference assistance. Most are not trained in archival research and many work under time constraints. They may be paid on an hourly basis or work for an employer with a deadline, or both. Reporters, both print and television, epitomize the deadline problem. Professional users, expecting to find ready reference collections or detailed indexes that will answer their questions quickly, may be disconcerted when they must instead search through materials scattered in many records. For example, information needed by a historic preservation architect to preserve a building usually is not in one folder, but must be assembled from unpublished and published sources, including city directories, maps, tax records, building permits, photograph collections, and newspapers.

In the past, some professional users were denied access to archives. By requiring scholarly credentials of users, many repositories denied access to

[12] William L. Joyce, "Archivists and Research Use," *American Archivist* 47 (Spring 1984): 124-33; *Toward A Usable Past: Historical Records in the Empire State* (Albany: New York State Archives, 1984).

[13] Robert Brent Toplin, "Introduction: Movie Reviews," *Journal of American History* 76 (December 1989): 1004. *San Francisco Examiner* 14 October 1990, C-1; and 30 December 1990, E-3.

other types of users, including professional users. Today, archival and manuscript repositories strive to define access as broadly as possible since professional users put information from archives to work in the real world and affect public policy in important ways.

3. Scholars. Scholars are a primary vocational constituency for research repositories. As direct users of archives, scholars transmit and transfer historical information from archival sources to the indirect users of archives. Although many think that historians are the most frequent users of archives, scholars from numerous disciplines use archival holdings: geography, political science, demography, sociology, literature, medicine, epidemiology, among others. It is also important to note that scholars may not always be affiliated with academic institutions; independent scholars are found in many fields, and avocational researchers or genealogists may be scholars. Whatever their field, scholars are more likely to be interpretive rather than factual researchers, with research of broad scope.

Scholars disseminate archival information to many indirect users. (*Peter Galfas, courtesy of Oral History Research Office, Columbia University*)

Research in archives calls for a partnership between archivists and researchers, but the relationship between archivists and scholars has not always been as smooth as might be expected from their shared goals. Although archivists generally assume that scholars are skilled in historical research, courses in research methodologies are no longer taught in many history departments, and other disciplines may lack specific historical knowledge and research training. Changes in research methodology and changes in the nature of archival sources have affected the relationship between archivists and scholars. Access restrictions limiting the use of recent materials also have been a source of disagreement among scholars and archivists.[14]

Reference archivists need to understand the nature of scholarly inquiry, research methodologies, and use of archival evidence in all disciplines using the archives. Even advanced scholars sometimes need assistance with intellectual aspects of their research, and, as discussed in the next chapter, in provenance-based systems, many users need archival mediation to translate subject requests into names of particular record groups and series. Archivists can assist scholars in evaluating archival information by sharing their knowledge of organizational activities and the technological processes that brought the documents into being.[15]

In many cases scholars are away from home and need to accomplish much research in a limited time. Consequently, they expect to handle a large quantity of material and request large numbers of photocopies. Notwithstanding their appreciation of the importance of documents, scholars do not always handle them with care. In their haste to "get through" great quantities of documents, they may be careless in using them. Indeed, one scholar described the "prosaic problem of obtaining maximum poundage of document inspection for a given hotel bill."[16]

Evidence indicates that scholars often learn about research sources through footnotes and bibli-

[14] Walter Rundell, Jr., *In Pursuit of American History: Research and Training in the United States* (Norman: University of Oklahoma Press, 1970); Fredric Miller, "Use, Appraisal, and Research: A Case Study of Social History," *American Archivist* 49 (Fall 1986): 371-92; Dale C. Mayer, "The New Social History: Implications for Archivists," *American Archivist* 48 (Fall 1985): 388-99; Alonzo L. Hamby and Edward Weldon, *Access to Papers of Recent Public Figures: The New Harmony Conference* (Bloomington, Ind.: Organization of American Historians, 1977).

[15] Stephen E. Wiberley, Jr., and William G. Jones, "Patterns of Information Seeking in the Humanities," *College and Research Libraries* 50 (November 1989): 638-45.

[16] Laurence R. Veysey, "A Scholar's View of University Archives," *College and University Archives: Selected Readings* (Chicago: Society of American Archivists), 154.

ographies in monographs and journals and through conversation in informal networks.[17] This is not surprising, since previous scholars' use of material is a clearer indication of relevance than any index or catalog. Archivists can become part of scholarly networks by participating in conferences and learned societies and by writing about archival sources in journals and newsletters of scholarly associations. The entry of archival sources in national databases such as OCLC (Online Computer Library Center) and RLIN (Research Libraries Information Network) promises to make more information about archival holdings available everywhere. Organizing means to make these databases readily available and teaching potential users to use them are pressing professional tasks.

In addition to serving individual scholars, repositories can serve as intellectual centers for scholarship. They can organize roundtables and seminars to discuss research in progress; such forums are useful for archivists as well as scholars. Repositories may sponsor conferences for scholars and archivists to discuss research trends or common concerns about documentation. Some well-endowed repositories offer grants-in-aid to assist scholars with travel and other research costs.

4. Students. Not all academic research is conducted by mature scholars. For many repositories, particularly university archives and manuscript libraries on or near college campuses, students are a major constituency. Archivists have an important opportunity to help students appreciate historical documents and archival institutions. Although most students will not become professional historians, as citizens they should learn to appreciate the value of history and the institutions that preserve it.

Archives help make history come alive for young people. Most students experience history primarily through thoroughly digested and neatly packaged textbook accounts. Most of them, like the general public, respond enthusiastically to the authenticity of original source materials. Historical documents, as artifacts, engage their senses and challenge them to respond. Historical documents can be illustration, but more importantly, can be evidence that provokes questions and stimulates hypotheses. Working with documents demonstrates the complex reality of the past. If properly guided through archival research, students can be stimu-

Young users study documents in a private research center. (*Lester Sullivan, courtesy of Amistad Research Center*)

lated to think more analytically and to look for the connections between past and present.

In some ways, the enthusiasm and excitement that students bring to research can make working with them very rewarding, but student questions frequently are repetitive, simplistic, or naive. Busy reference archivists may find it difficult to muster enthusiasm for yet another term paper on the frontier experience, gold rush, or Depression. As William Maher notes, students can be "high volume users that place heavy demands on the program but whose use generally touches only the surface of the archives and utilizes only the simplest techniques of historical research."[18]

Planning reference services for students requires awareness of the types of assistance needed. A doctoral student writing a dissertation presents different demands than does a high school or elementary student. An exceptional student who independently identifies a subject calling for archival resources requires a different degree of assistance than the more usual case of a class of students sent to the archives with instructions to use primary sources for a term paper.

If the research experience is not structured, students can be overwhelmed by research in archives. They frequently need help in adapting topics to available time and sources. For example, a proposed term paper on the Depression may need to be focused on a narrower topic such as a university's response to government work programs for students. Students usually appreciate suggestions for manage-

---

[17] Margaret Steig, "The Information of [sic] Needs of Historians," *College and Research Libraries* 42 (November 1981): 544-60; Michael E. Stevens, "The Historian and Archival Finding Aids," *Georgia Archive* 5 (Winter 1977): 64-74.

[18] I am grateful to William Maher for sharing an early draft of his manual, *College and University Archives* (Chicago: Society of American Archivists, forthcoming).

able term paper topics. In many cases, the archivist also may need to recommend preliminary or background reading. Students also need help in understanding and evaluating the mass of information in documents and assistance with the difficult task of generalizing intelligently from details.

The educational role of the reference archivist is perhaps most obvious in work with students, but working with students is in many ways similar to working with other unskilled researchers, although other users usually have defined their needs more precisely than most students writing an assigned term paper. Experienced archivists have learned that many students need no more assistance than other users who are not particularly skilled in archival research or who bring complex research projects requiring considerable reference time.

It is usually not the complexity of teaching students, but their numbers that pose difficulties for repositories. Most repositories can provide reference services for occasional students with well-defined questions, but most do not have adequate resources to respond to large classes with poorly defined needs. It can be a joy to work with a motivated, well-prepared student. Unprepared, reluctant students are likely to find little pleasure or value in using archival resources and will be more likely to create problems for the archivist.

Providing these educational services to students depends in part on the mission of the parent institution. Teaching any unskilled user is time-consuming, and some archivists hesitate to commit scarce staff resources to it. Often the parent institution does not recognize the educational role of archives, even in academic settings. Academic archivists generally feel obliged to teach students because of the instructional role of their parent institution. Participating in bibliographic instruction programs offered by college and university libraries can reach many students. In repositories that must limit services for students, problems may be forestalled if the access policy states that a student must have a letter of introduction from an instructor.

5. Teachers. Many of the problems encountered in working with students are better resolved by working directly with their teachers. Ideally, archives are a laboratory for research in the social sciences, and archivists and teachers work together to instruct students in historical research. A successful collaboration requires much effort. By working with an instructor, the archivist may be better able to understand and meet the goals of the assignment, and also develop means to save staff time. Most

Researched and written by Education Branch staff, National Archives

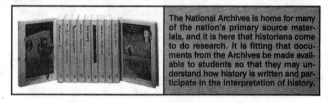

Facsimile documents kits are attractive and stimulating teaching tools. *(SIRS National Archives Documents)*

teachers have an idea of what they want their students to gain from archival research, but many do not know what services to expect from archives, as few have used primary source materials themselves. In addition, many may not perceive archivists as fellow educators willing to share research skills. Some teachers believe in the "sink or swim" method of learning research skills, and archivists may need tact and diplomacy to impress on teachers the importance of structuring the research experience and of making it an integral part of the course of study. It is the instructor's responsibility to develop background reading, request intermediate outlines and bibliographies, and discuss research in progress. They can work with archivists to identify workable topics and to discuss techniques for reading and understanding historical documents. Archivists can help students by discussing their progress with instructors. By reviewing student papers and projects, archivists can

Teachers use historical documents to bring history alive for young people. (*New York State Archives and Records Administration*)

learn what difficulties the students encountered and can assist teachers in improving the use of archives in the future.

Public programs and publications are often effective ways to meet the needs of students, as well as other groups of unskilled users. For example, more can be accomplished in a one-hour introductory orientation class than in hours working with individual students. Structured orientation sessions are usually more successful than tours. Class sessions work best when instructors attend with the students so that they also understand the archivist's objectives and presentation.

A well-prepared orientation session, focused on the subject area of the course and supplemented with handouts on repository procedures and research, can prepare students for productive work in the repository as well as stimulate a general understanding of and appreciation for archival research. Providing examples of research projects, reading vivid passages from documents, showing photographs, and illustrating the use of original sources bring the research process alive. Demonstrating use of finding aids, proper care of materials, procedures for requesting materials and photocopies, and methods of taking notes and citing materials can save time and effort for both students and archivists.

If education is a high priority in the archival mission, as is especially likely in college and university archives, approaching faculty with a list of potential research topics or resources and offering to lead an orientation session, preferably in the archives, are means to extend the archival mission. Reviewing course catalogs and schedules can identify courses for which the resources of the archives

might be beneficial. Repositories looking for potential users should not overlook neighboring community colleges, which are unlikely to have extensive archival holdings. The Organization of American Historians (OAH) estimates that more than thirty percent of all history enrollments are in community colleges.[19]

Archivists and teachers can also work together to locate suitable documents and other primary sources to enhance classroom lectures or discussion. Facsimile documents are a proven method of reaching high school and elementary classes. Reproductions of historical documents for classroom exhibits, slide-tape shows, videos, filmstrips, or teaching packets can, if well done, enhance learning and bring historical events to life.[20]

Avocational Users. Archives can play a significant role in educating the general public. A recent study of humanities in the United States found that institutions such as libraries, museums, and historical societies are flourishing because the American public is hungry for personal connections to the past.[21] An earlier study noted that "personal engagement with history marks a fruitful path toward self-knowledge."[22] Many people who found classroom history boring and alienating search eagerly for a personal, usable past. Sometimes archivists seem surprised by requests from avocational researchers such as genealogists, amateur historians, and hobbyists. They may seem less important or less justifiable in face of pressing needs. That researchers find joy in archival research should not be surprising, however, for it is such intangible rewards that brought many archivists to the field as a vocation.

In a pluralistic society it is important for individuals, families, and groups to have a sense of time, place, and identity. As the OAH states, "all people have been significant actors in human events ... history is not limited to the study of dominant political, social, and economic elites.... It also encom-

[19] *OAH Newsletter* (February 1990): 2.

[20] Hugh Taylor, "Clio in the Raw: Archival Materials and the Teaching of History," *American Archivist* 35 (July/October 1972): 317-30; Kathleen Roe, *Teaching with Historical Records* (Albany: State Education Department, 1981); *Teaching with Documents: Using Primary Sources From the National Archives* (Washington, D. C.: National Archives, 1989); Mark A. Greene, "Using College and University Archives as Instructional Materials," *Midwestern Archivist* 14 (1989): 31-38.

[21] Lynne Cheney, *Humanities in America* (Washington, D. C.: National Endowment for the Humanities, 1988); see also Richard H. Kohn, "The Future of the Historical Profession," American Historical Association *Perspectives,* 27 (November 1989): 8-12.

[22] *The Humanities in American Life* (Berkeley: University of California Press, 1980), 137.

Genealogical information from archives is often shared at family reunions. (*Robert Holsinger, courtesy of Jonathan R. Stayer Collection, York, Pennsylvania*)

passes the individual and collective quests of ordinary people for a meaningful place for themselves in their families, in their communities, and in the larger world."[23] Memory, both personal and cultural, is critical to a sense of identity.

1. Genealogists. Many Americans seek meaningful connections with the past through family history. Genealogy, one of the most popular hobbies in America, appeals to all economic, racial, and ethnic groups. The 1977 television movie *Roots,* based on the best seller by Alex Haley, is often cited as the motivating factor in the recent explosion of interest in genealogy. Many archivists, however, will testify that *Roots* was only the most visible manifestation of an already well-developed phenomenon. Genealogists often share the results of their research with other family members and have wide-ranging and sophisticated interests and research skills.

Because the direct impact of genealogy beyond individuals is not easily measured and because of its

past association with elitist patriotic societies, its value may be discounted or dismissed as idle curiosity. In some repositories, genealogists are not considered qualified researchers and are denied access; in others they are tolerated yet not encouraged, but in many they are welcomed. For many repositories, genealogists are the most numerous clientele, even though they may not be identified or recognized in the institutional mission statement. Genealogists can be a valuable constituency for archival agencies, especially government archives and historical societies, because they are numerous and vocal about the value of preserving historical records. Their numbers help justify allocation of increased resources to reference operations.[24]

---

[23] *OAH Newsletter* (February 1991): 6.

[24] Phebe R. Jacobsen, " 'The World Turned Upside Down': Reference Priorities and the State Archives," *American Archivist* 44 (Fall 1981): 341-45; Peter W. Bunce, "Towards a More Harmonious Relationship: A Challenge to Archivists and Genealogists," and Elizabeth Shown Mills, "Genealogists and Archivists: Communicating, Cooperating, and Coping!" *SAA Newsletter* (May 1990).

Pamphlets and guides assist genealogical research. (*Pennsylvania Historical and Museum Commission*)

As in the case of perceived problems in dealing with students, it is usually the number of unskilled genealogists that present problems for understaffed archives, not the nature of the inquiry. Because their information needs are often simpler and more predictable than those of other constituencies, archivists have good opportunities to serve them effectively through educational programs and self-help devices. Pamphlets, brochures, and other handouts can explain the use of commonly used sources. Many how-to books are available. Instructional videotapes make information about using archives readily available and can be shown to groups outside the archives. Microfilming frequently requested materials and placing copies of heavily consulted sources on open shelves can expedite reference services.

Archives can work with genealogical societies to develop educational programs. Classes that teach genealogical research skills are well attended. Experienced genealogists can be trained as volunteers to help novices. Genealogical societies also are a source of volunteers to index commonly used sources such as censuses, cemetery records, and newspapers.

2. Historians. Prominent examples of avocational historians are local historians and hobbyists. Like genealogists, their interests reflect a modern society's need for a usable past. Interest in local history is often stimulated by community celebrations and anniversaries. These may focus on the community as a whole or on its many parts: churches, civic groups, businesses, schools, labor unions, ethnic groups, hospitals, or other institutions. Home owners or business owners seek information about the history of their building or company. To show their involvement in the community, local businesses of-ten use archival resources in marketing or public relations, in much the same way that large businesses turn to their own archives.

Few community organizations have organized their own archives, and they may recognize the value of archives only when they try to find them to use in celebrating their past. This interest in archives provides the opportunity to offer records management and archival advice. In many cases, anniversaries motivate organizations to deposit their historical materials with a suitable collecting agency, such as a county historical society or manuscripts library, and to institute a records program.

Lectures, classes, exhibitions, and publications can help local historians. A lecture series provides a forum for historians and other community members to communicate the results of archival research, presents information about the community to citizens unable to undertake their own research, and provides a showcase for repository resources and services. Exhibitions, either within the repository or in other public forums, present information about the community and encourage use. Slide shows or videotapes can be shown in classrooms or at civic meetings. A column in the local paper, well-illustrated by historical photographs, can stimulate community interest and teach research skills. If a community celebration is underway, orientation classes to teach research skills lessen the need for individual orientations by reference staff.

Hobbyists find meaning in the past by focusing on selected objects and events from the past. For almost any common object one can name, there is a group devoted to its preservation and history: trains, ships, lighthouses, bottles, circuses, automobiles, carousels, prospecting, and military engagements. Hobbyists come to archives to search for documentary evidence about the history of their interest, or to ensure authentic restoration or reenactment. Because of their intense interest, hobbyists can produce perhaps greatest reference pressure of any user group. They are often collectors themselves and sometimes locate valuable historical records still in private hands. If they are impressed with a repository's care of records and service to researchers, they may recommend the repository to private owners of historical materials.

* * *

Many people come to archives in search of historical information. Some seek information for their work—administrative staff, archivists, professional users, scholars, students, and teachers; others for personal interest—genealogists, amateur historians, and hobbyists. Some researchers are experienced in archival research while others are novices. Some seek facts to solve particular problems, others mold interpretation for broad publics. The products of archival research include publications, reports, films, family histories, and personal satisfaction.

Reference services, access policies, and public programs must be designed to meet these varied needs for intellectual, legal, and physical access. Researchers rely on finding aids and reference assistance to locate the information to answer their questions. The next two chapters will discuss the means by which archivists assist users to meet their needs and to answer their questions.

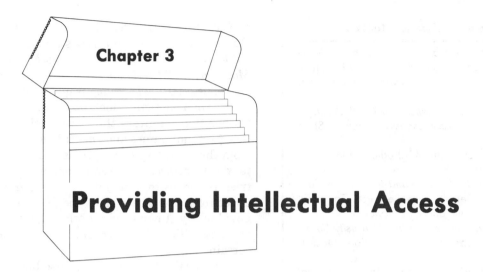

Chapter 3

Providing Intellectual Access

Providing intellectual access to the holdings of archival and manuscript repositories is a fundamental task for reference service. Archivists provide five types of intellectual access:

1) information about the repository,
2) information about holdings,
3) information from holdings,
4) information about records creators, and
5) referrals to sources outside the repository.

Most repositories acknowledge a professional obligation to provide information about themselves and their holdings through national directories, repository publications, and public programs. More detailed information about holdings is provided internally through unpublished inventories, registers, card catalogs, indexes, and in-house databases; it is provided externally through repository guides, published finding aids, specialized publications, national guides, and bibliographic databases.

Researchers often need reference assistance to make effective use of these tools. Since the role of the reference archivist in providing intellectual access in large measure depends on the repository's program of arrangement and description and the available finding aids, this chapter will discuss common reference tools and finding aid systems.[1] It will also discuss the role of the reference archivist in providing intellectual access to the three other types of information: information from repository holdings, information about records creators, and referrals to sources outside the repository.

Information about Repositories

Every repository, regardless of size, has an obligation to provide information about itself so that users can find it. Contributing to directories is one means, and every repository should ensure that it is listed in appropriate national and regional directories. Major reference tools are listed in Figure 3-1. In addition to disseminating information about their own repository, reference archivists often use such reference tools to make referrals beyond the repository. Information about the repository can also be provided through publications and public programs.

1. Directories. The most important directory of archival repositories is the *Directory of Archives and Manuscript Repositories in the United States,* compiled by the National Historical Publications and Records Commission and frequently referred to as the NHPRC *Directory.* The only national listing for all kinds of archives and manuscript repositories, the *Directory* provides entries for 4,225 repositories in the United States, Puerto Rico, and the Virgin Islands. Entries are arranged alphabetically by state, within each state by city, and then by repository. As seen in Figure 3-2, each entry provides name of repository, address, telephone number, hours, copying facilities, a brief statement of repository collecting policy, and total quantity, inclusive dates,

---

[1] For discussion of the principles underlying archival finding aids—provenance, original order, hierarchy of control, collective description, and progressive refinement of control—see Fredric Miller, *Arranging and Describing Archives and Manuscripts* (Chicago: Society of American Archivists: 1990).

Figure 3-1   National Reference Tools

Directory of Archives and Manuscript Repositories in the United States, compiled by the National Historical Publications and Records Commission. 2nd edition. Phoenix: Oryx Press, 1988.

Directory of Historical Agencies in North America. 14th edition. Nashville: American Association for State and Local History, 1990.

American Library Directory. 43rd edition. New York: R. R. Bowker, 1990-1991.

Directory of Special Libraries and Information Centers. 14th edition. Detroit: Gale Research Company, 1991. Supplement, *New Special Libraries.*

Special Collections in College and University Libraries, compiled by Modoc Press, Inc. New York: Macmillan, 1989.

Picture Researcher's Handbook: An International Guide to Picture Sources, compiled by Hilary and Mary Evans. 3rd edition. Wokingham, Berkshire: Van Nostrand Reinhold, 1986.

An Index to American Photographic Collections, compiled at the International Museum of Photography at George Eastman House by James McQuaid, editor. Boston: G. K. Hall, 1982.

Footage 89: North American Film and Video Sources, edited by Richard Prelinger and Celeste R. Hoffnar. New York: Prelinger Associates, 1989.

Encyclopedia of Information Systems and Services, John Schmittroth, Jr., editor. 10th edition. Detroit: Gale Research, 1990. Supplement *New Information Systems and Services.*

National Union Catalog of Manuscript Collections. Washington: Library of Congress, 1959—.

Index to Personal Names in the National Union Catalog of Manuscript Collections 1959-1984 compiled by Harriet Ostroff. Alexandria, Va.: Chadwyck-Healey, 1988.

Richard C. Davis, *North American Forest History: A Guide to Archives and Manuscripts in the United States and Canada.* Santa Barbara, CA: Clio Books, 1977.

Women's History Sources, edited by Andrea Hinding, et al. New York: Bowker, 1979.

American Literary Manuscripts: A Checklist of Holdings in Academic, Historical, Public Libraries, Museums, and Authors' Homes in the United States. Athens: University of Georgia Press, 1977.

National Inventory of Documentary Sources in the United States. Alexandria, Va. : Chadwyck-Healey.

OCLC
    Online Computer Library Center
    6565 Frantz Road, Dublin, OH 43017-0702
    (800) 848-5878

RLIN
    Research Libraries Group
    1200 Villa Street, Mountain View, CA 94041
    (415) 962-9951 or (800) 537-7546

and brief narrative description of holdings. Also included are citations for repository guides, subject guides, and entries in the *National Union Catalog of Manuscript Collections.*

The NHPRC *Directory* is most useful for finding records of a particular locality or the records of institutions that maintain their own archives. An index lists personal names and geographical terms derived from the narrative descriptions and offers rudimentary subject access. A repository index lists all entries by repository name. The *Directory* was produced from a database using the SPINDEX program, now largely superseded by other database systems; the possibility of future editions is therefore uncertain.

Several other directories also list archival and manuscript repositories, though none as extensively as the NHPRC *Directory.* The *Directory of Historical Agencies in North America,* published by the American Association for State and Local History, contains listings of local historical societies and museums, genealogical societies, oral history centers, folklore societies, and living history groups, as well as archives and manuscript repositories. The 1990 edition lists some 13,000 historical agencies. The brief entries give only location and a general description of repository holdings.

Library directories include some archival and manuscript repositories. The *American Library Directory* appears annually and lists public, academic, governmental, and special libraries in the United States and Canada; entries are arranged geographically. Each entry includes name, address, names of key staff, and information on holdings, including special collections such as manuscripts or archives. The *Directory of Special Libraries and Information Centers* is a comprehensive guide to more than 19,800 special libraries, research libraries, information centers, archives, and data centers, listed in one alphabetical sequence. A subject index identifies major fields of interest for each repository. A periodic supplement, *New Special Libraries,* updates the directory between editions.

There are also a number of specialized directories that describe and locate repositories. *Special Collections in College and University Libraries* describes 1,800 repositories that collect rare books, personal manuscripts, and other specialized collections. The *Picture Researcher's Handbook: An International Guide to Picture Sources,* compiled by Hilary and Mary Evans, lists many archival and manuscript repositories with significant visual holdings. Another source of repositories holding photographs

Figure 3-2 *Directory of Archives and Manuscript Repositories in the United States*

SEE ALSO: Alan M. Meckler and Ruth McMullin, comps., *Oral History Collections* (Bowker, 1975); Willa K. Baum, 'Oral History: A Revived Tradition at the Bancroft Library.' *Pacific Northwest Quarterly* 58 (April 1967); 'History on Tape: The Regional Oral History Office at the Bancroft Library,' *California Historical Quarterly* 54 (Spring 1975).

CA86-815

University of California, Berkeley
The Bancroft Library
University Archives
281 Library
Berkeley CA 94720

(415) 642-2933

OPEN: M-F 9-5; closed weekends and holidays
COPYING FACILITIES: yes
MATERIALS SOLICITED: Manuscripts, photographs, tape recordings, and memorabilia relating to the University of California.

HOLDINGS:
Total volume: 9,000,000 items
Inclusive dates: 1855 -
Description: Records of the University of California from its inception in 1868, and documentation generated by its predecessor, the College of California. Included are office files, Academic Senate records, student and alumni publications, photographs, memorabilia, and printed materials. Also held are records of the systemwide administration of the University and of the Berkeley campus, as well as materials concerning other campuses in the University of California system.

CA86-820

University of California, Berkeley
Department of Architecture
313A Wurster Hall
Berkeley CA 94720

(415) 642-5124

OPEN: variable hours
ACCESS: advance arrangements advised
COPYING FACILITIES: yes
MATERIALS SOLICITED: Material related to architecture and landscape architecture in California.

HOLDINGS:
Total volume: 1,500,000 items
Inclusive dates: 1885 -
Description: Consists of 30,000 architectural drawings for California, as well as landscape architectural drawings for California, the eastern United States, and England. Also included are 1,000,000 blueprints for the San Francisco Bay area and the William W. Wurster collection of architectural drawings, photographs, and papers. Collections of private papers of California architects include those of Bernard Maybeck, Charles Sumner Green, Julia Morgan, John Galen Howard, Willis Polk, and the landscape architects Beatrix Farrand and Gertrude Jekyll.

CA86-850

University of California, Berkeley
Forestry Library
The Metcalf-Fritz Photograph
  Collection
260 Mulford Hall
Berkeley CA 94720

(415) 642-2936

OPEN: M-Th 9-9, F 9-5, Sa, Su 1-5; summer, M-F 9-5; closed holidays, and weekends in summer
COPYING FACILITIES: yes
MATERIALS SOLICITED: Photographs which show forestry activities in California, particularly those associated with the University's Department of Forestry and Conservation.

HOLDINGS:
Total volume: 36 l.f.
Inclusive dates: 1910 -
Description: Over 8,000 photographs (many with matching negatives) illustrating logging equipment, logging operations, reforestation, lumber mills, specimens of tree species, and activities of the University of California's School of Forestry. Most of the photographs were taken in California. About 20 percent concern forestry in other parts of the United States (particularly Oregon and Washington), and there are some pictures of logging in Europe during World War I.

SEE: Davis.

CA86-882

University of California, Berkeley
Lawrence Berkeley Laboratory
Archives and Records
1 Cyclotron Road
Building 69-107
Berkeley CA 94720

(415) 486-5525

OPEN: M-F 8-4; closed weekends and holidays
COPYING FACILITIES: yes
MATERIALS SOLICITED: Official administrative and research records of Lawrence Berkeley Laboratory, including papers of noteworthy scientists; business records of the Manhattan Engineering District; and records reflecting interdisciplinary group research, particularly in physics, nuclear science, and medical physics.

HOLDINGS:
Total volume: 15,000 c.f.
Inclusive dates: 1941 -
Description: Records of Lawrence Berkeley Laboratory, including Director's Office documents, business records, division and department files, and individual scientist files. Included are correspondence, photographs, official files, magnetic tapes, film containing raw data, and drawings. The records relate to basic research at the Laboratory and reflect the relationship of science to government and to the University.

CA86-890

University of California, Berkeley
Music Library
240 Morrison Hall
Berkeley CA 94720

(415) 642-2623

OPEN: M-Th 9-9, F, Sa 9-5, Su 1-5; summer and semester breaks, M-F 9-5; closed holidays
ACCESS: an appointment is advised
COPYING FACILITIES: yes
MATERIALS SOLICITED: Manuscripts of so-called Western art music and music treatises dating from the Middle Ages to the present which have demonstrable research value for musicologists.

HOLDINGS:
Total volume: 250 l.f.
Inclusive dates: 11th century -
Description: More than 2,000 volumes of musical scores and treatises (11th century-19th century); 250 music manuscripts by 20th century composers such as Ernst Bloch, Sigmund Romberg, Darius Milhaud, Luigi Dallapiccola, and local composers of the San Francisco Bay area; musicological papers of Manfred Bukofzer and Alfred Einstein; and the correspondence, diaries, and musical compositions of Alfred Hertz, conductor of the San Francisco Symphony Orchestra. There is also a sound archive of 22,000 78 rpm discs.

SEE: Spalek.

SEE ALSO: Vincent Duckles and Minnie Elmer, *Thematic Catalog of a Manuscript Collection of Eighteenth-Century Italian Instrumental Music in the University of California, Berkeley, Music Library* (Univ. of California Press, 1963).

CA86-895

University of California, Berkeley
Office for History of Science and
  Technology
Archive for History of Quantum
  Physics
470 Stephens Hall
Berkeley CA 94720

(415) 642-4581

OPEN: M-F 9-5; closed weekends and holidays
COPYING FACILITIES: yes

HOLDINGS:
Total volume: 317 microfilms
Inclusive dates: 1898 - 1933
Description: A microfilm collection of primary source materials for the study of the history of quantum physics, including letters, manuscripts, notebooks, and personal commentaries of major physicists.

SEE ALSO: Thomas S. Kuhn, John L Heilbron, Paul Forman, and Lini Allen, *Sources for the History of Quantum Physics: An Inventory and Report* (1967).

is *An Index to American Photographic Collections,* compiled at the International Museum of Photography at George Eastman House by James McQuaid. Film sources are described in *Footage 89: North American Film and Video Sources,* edited by Richard Prelinger and Celeste R. Hoffnar. Repositories holding electronic records are listed in the *Encyclopedia of Information Systems and Services,* John Schmittroth, Jr., editor; this is updated by periodic supplements entitled *New Information Systems and Services.*

2. Repository Publications. Repositories publish brochures, pamphlets, and other handouts to convey general information about themselves. Such publications save reference staff time by answering frequently asked questions about access, holdings, and services. They can be sent in response to requests for information and distributed at meetings and in libraries and other locations accessible to potential users. They also can help educate administrators in the parent institution and actual and potential donors.

A general repository brochure should include both administrative and descriptive information. Practical matters such as location, hours of operation, access policy, information about public transportation to the repository, parking, and handicapped access, should be explained. The availability of specialized reference and copying services should be mentioned, a telephone number given for additional information, and, if appropriate, a fax or e-mail number. A repository brochure also should describe generally the holdings and types of uses that they can support. A summary of the collecting policy is helpful to potential donors and users, as is a list of subjects.

Reference staff should help prepare repository brochures. Depending on the nature of the holdings and user interest, reference staff also can prepare supplemental brochures describing particular bodies of records or areas of inquiry, such as sources and services for genealogical or pictorial research.

3. Public Programs. Many other activities can be used to disseminate information about a repository. Reference staff can help to identify constituencies of current and potential users and develop programs to reach them. Such outreach activities as speeches, exhibitions, publications, audio-visual presentations, videotapes, tours, and festivals inform potential users about archival resources and how to use them.

Information about Holdings

Archivists disseminate information about repository holdings in two ways. Within the repository such information is provided through unpublished finding aids, such as inventories, registers, card catalogs, indexes, and in-house databases. Outside the repository information about holdings is provided through published repository guides and national reference tools.

1. In-house Finding Aids. In an ideal world, archival descriptive systems would be designed after assessing the needs of users. Instead, most archivists and curators inherit finding aids from previous eras in the life of the repository. These often reflect the influence of tradition, an evolving mixture of styles, and an earlier lack of descriptive standards.

Generally, two types of finding aid systems evolved in the United States: provenance-based descriptive systems and content-indexing descriptive systems. In provenance-based systems, descriptive information "derives only from what is known about the file—the activities of the creating person or organization and the structure or organizing principles of the file itself." Such systems developed primarily in institutional archives. In content-indexing systems, derived from librarianship, "information is gleaned by an indexer who examines the records." These systems were more likely to develop in manuscript repositories.[2] Let us look more closely at each of these types.

a. Evolution of Provenance-based Descriptive Systems in Archives. The organization and retrieval of archival materials in provenance-based systems rest on very simple premises, growing from the creation and use of information in the creating organization. Consider for a moment the organization and use of information in a complex modern institution. In the course of work, staff members receive and send information, some of which is captured in documents. Some documents, like rules and directives, flow downward to communicate orders and instruction. Others, like reports, flow upward to give managers information needed to control money, labor, and materials. Still other documents, like memoranda, communicate laterally to coordinate activities and share information needed by more than one department. Thus, organizational activities

² Richard Lytle, "Intellectual Access to Archives: Provenance and Content Indexing Methods of Subject Retrieval," *American Archivist* 43 (Winter 1980): 64. See also David Bearman and Richard Lytle, "The Power of the Principle of Provenance," *Archivaria* 21 (1985-1986): 14-27.

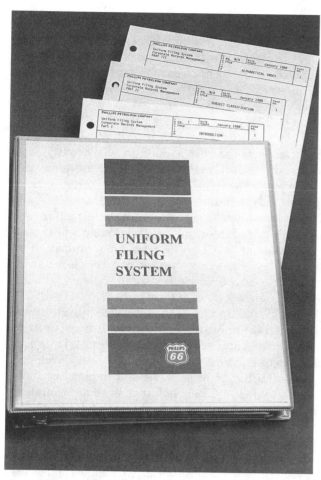

Companywide user manuals guide retrieval of information in corporate files. (*Greg Booker, courtesy of Phillips Petroleum Company*)

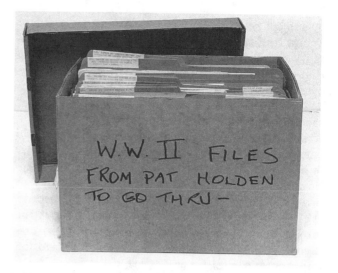

Archivists maintain provenance and original order of records transferred to archives. (*Greg Booker, courtesy of Phillips Petroleum Company*)

generate documents that collect in files maintained where the information is needed in the course of daily business; department files reflect the activities that generate them.[3]

Staff find information in current files through knowledge of an organization's activities and its filing systems. An employee summons knowledge of the organization and its functions to infer what person or department would collect the desired information. Such knowledge may come from personal experience or other staff members, or it may be set forth in standard practice manuals, organization charts, or staff directories. Organizational employees (and their clients or customers outside the organization) find information by asking, "Who is responsible? Who keeps that information?" Information about

the forms in which information is recorded and filed may be obtained from clerical staff, filing procedures codified in filing manuals, or through filing guides or indexes maintained by clerical staff.

The same principles of organization and retrieval hold true for records after they move from active to archival status. Archivists retain the provenance and original order of the files; that is, records from each creating entity are kept together in the original order imposed by the creating department. They describe the functions and activities of the creating agency, and the forms, filing structures, and dates of its records. Since records are generated by activity, information can be found, without extensive indexing, by analyzing organizational structure and function to infer the location of files likely to hold needed information. These files are then searched by their internal structures. For example, by knowing form and source, one can infer the probable content of minutes of the governing board of a university or of scrapbooks of the advertising department of a bank.

Provenance-based arrangement systems are not bound by time or subject. Unlike subject-based classification schemes, the relationship between activities and records remains constant, no matter how later users approach the records. Indexes or file guides developed by creators are equally useful for later researchers. Records resulting from activities of large modern offices may reflect thousands of subjects. The records of a United States senator, for example, contain information about every significant issue during his tenure. Indexing such records

[3] The best history of organizational communication, information flows, information technology, and document forms is found in JoAnne Yates, *Control Through Communication: The Rise of System in American Management* (Baltimore: Johns Hopkins University Press, 1989).

by subject requires hours of staff time; yet if a user knows that the senator was involved in tobacco liability cases, it is possible to locate information on that topic by using the internal structure of the files, even though the collection has not been indexed.

As time passes, however, this straightforward scheme becomes more complex. Organizational structures evolve, functions and forms change, and personal and institutional memories fade. Outsiders or new staff with little or no knowledge of the institution may be the most numerous users. The farther users are from the activities that created the records, the more they need detailed information about the circumstances under which the records were created, and the more they rely on archival description and reference assistance.

To cope with the masses of modern governmental and institutional records, archivists devised methods of collective description to describe groups of records arranged by provenance. In the 1930s, building on European models, the National Archives, exemplifying what Richard Berner calls the public archives tradition, developed the inventory as its basic descriptive tool. This became an important model for other institutions. Usually prepared for each major creating agency, an inventory describes the activities and functions of the record creators in an administrative history, and summarizes the forms and arrangement of the records in series descriptions. Most inventories include only minimal information about the subjects of the records.[4]

To provide integrated intellectual access to all records described in inventories, archives published guides describing their holdings. The guide indexed names, places, and subjects. In theory, users first consulted the guide to identify records of interest and then used the inventories to locate specific series of interest. In practice, however, guides failed to cope with ever-changing record holdings and new inventories, and could not provide sufficient depth of indexing to meet the need for subject access.

Thus, in most archival repositories the reference archivist was, and still is, a critical element in making provenance-based systems work, for the archivist links subject requests with archival materials. Knowledge of the functional and administrative structure of the agencies producing records is necessary to develop a search strategy. The reference archivist helps a user link a topic with relevant sources by identifying the functions of records creators, locates the relevant finding aids, and identifies series likely to contain needed information. That is, the archivist helps the user answer a series of questions, "Who would have needed the information initially? How would they have recorded it? Where are the files now? How is the information filed?"[5]

An analysis of reference work at the National Archives suggests that archivists rely heavily on a personal "institutional memory" built on their experience and knowledge of the Archives' organization, finding aids, administrative histories, and rules-of-thumb about how to search specific holdings for particular kinds of information. The system works best when users are staff of the creating organization or subject specialists, because they can associate names of participating organizations and individuals with events and subjects of interest.[6]

b. Evolution of Content-indexing Descriptive Systems in Manuscript Repositories. Collecting personal papers or institutional records from outside sources, manuscript repositories developed other methods of organizing and describing their holdings. Many of their holdings were not complete collections. Institutional archives held by manuscript repositories were removed from the context of the creating organization, and personal papers often lacked the structural integrity of organizational archives. Since original order often was lost, holdings were arranged by subject, form, or chronology.

Therefore, many manuscript repositories developed descriptive systems based on content-indexing, cataloging systems that Richard Berner has called the historical manuscripts tradition. Like the Library of Congress, such repositories typically described items by rules similar to those used to catalog books. Individual items were cataloged in card catalogs by author, recipient, date, and subject. Some manuscript repositories also used calendars, or abstracts of manuscript items arranged chronologically, to describe their holdings. With such detailed control, based on examination of each item, collection-level description seemed unnecessary. Information about provenance, records creators, and a collection as a whole existed in the curator's memory.

[4] Richard Berner, *Archival Theory and Practice in the United States: A Historical Analysis* (Seattle: University of Washington Press, 1983), 30.

[5] Mary Jo Pugh, "The Illusion of Omniscience: Subject Access and the Reference Archivist," *American Archivist* 45 (Winter 1982): 33-44.

[6] American Management Systems, "Methodology for Developing an Expert System for Information Retrieval at the National Archives and Records Administration," (Washington: National Archives, 1986).

Such catalogs and calendars worked reasonably well until the mid-twentieth century. Most repositories and collections were small; users could learn about a collection by quickly examining it. As collections grew larger, however, description at the item level proved too time-consuming to produce and too cumbersome to use. Some manuscript repositories published guides to provide collection-level description, but important information about collections was often difficult to find. Curators were needed to provide information about collections, just as archivists were needed in provenance-based systems to provide integrated subject access.

c. Current Finding Aid Systems. Today, most archives and manuscript repositories use a two-stage system to provide intellectual access. From the user's point of view, a card catalog, index, guide, or database is the primary finding aid. Researchers bring names or subject queries to identify collections or other sets of records of probable interest. This primary tool then refers users to inventories or registers, which provide information about the creators of the records and the structure and content of the records. These frequently provide lists of box or folder titles, which users scan to select particular boxes or folders of interest.

Descriptive systems ought to free users from dependence on archivists and curators and free archivists and curators from dependence on memory. It is dangerous to rely too heavily on the archivist's knowledge of subject or the curator's knowledge of provenance to provide intellectual access for users. The quality of reference service can vary from day to day as staff are absent from work, and from year to year as archivists change jobs, retire, or simply forget.

It is true, however, that no finding aid can address all future uses of the records and that novice users will need instruction and assistance no matter how complete the finding aids. It also may be that the more sophisticated the finding aids become, the more some users will require assistance to use them. Although knowledgeable reference archivists always will be needed, finding aids should capture their knowledge so that users can be as self sufficient as possible.

Gradually this goal is being realized as the public archives and historical manuscript traditions merge. Most manuscript repositories today describe collections in a register, which is similar to the archival inventory. Most archives now provide bridging tools as indexes to the inventories. Card catalogs, cumulative indexes, or published guides provide integrated, collection-level access. Today an automated database is increasingly likely to be the integrative tool in both settings.[7]

Archivists continue to explore integrative devices that provide both subject and provenance access. Modern information technologies and the MARC AMC format (*MA*chine-*R*eadable *C*ataloging *A*rchives and *M*anuscripts *C*ontrol) make both repository systems and national systems for access to information about archival and manuscript holdings real possibilities. Automating descriptive systems eventually may mean that users and other staff need not rely so heavily on the knowledge of reference archivists. Shared descriptive systems depend on standard formats for exchanging information, rules for describing archives and manuscripts, and authority control of indexing terms.[8]

Although much interest in recent years has focused on improving subject access to provenance-based systems, archivists are also exploring new methods to exploit the "power of provenance." They are using the provenance information contained in administrative histories and series descriptions to identify organizational functions and forms of materials that can be used as index terms in addition to subject headings. As David Bearman asserts, "Such a descriptive language for documented activities makes it possible to fulfill the obligation to locate documentation of accountability directly, rather than through circuitous inferences."[9]

Description traditionally has focused on *products*, the finding aids that give access to archival holdings. Today, archivists focus on the *process* of capturing information about records through the en-

[7] The term "bridging aids" comes from *Keeping Archives* (Sydney: Australian Society of Archivists, 1987), 164.

[8] Such standards are discussed in Nancy Sahli, *MARC for Archives and Manuscripts: The AMC Format* (Chicago: Society of American Archivists, 1985); Max J. Evans and Lisa B. Weber, *MARC for Archives and Manuscripts: A Compendium of Practice* (Madison: State Historical Society of Wisconsin, 1985); Steven L. Hensen, *Archives, Personal Papers, and Manuscripts: A Cataloging Manual* (Chicago: Society of American Archivists, 1989); Steven L. Hensen, "The Use of Standards in the Application of the AMC Format," *American Archivist* 49 (Winter 1986): 31-40; David Bearman, "Authority Control: Issues and Prospects," *American Archivist* 52 (Summer 1989): 286-300.

[9] David Bearman, "Archives and Manuscript Control With Bibliographic Utilities: Opportunities and Challenges," *American Archivist* 52 (Winter 1989): 33. See also Avra Michelson, "Description and Reference in the Age of Automation," *American Archivist* 50 (Spring 1987): 192-208; Alden Monroe and Kathleen Roe, "What's the Purpose? Functional Access to Archival Records," in *Beyond the Book: Extending MARC for Subject Access* (Boston: G. K. Hall, 1990), 157-70; Helena Zinkham, Patricia Cloud, and Hope Mayo, "Providing Access by Form of Material, Genre, and Physical Characteristics: Benefits and Techniques," *American Archivist* 52 (Summer 1989): 300-19.

tire life cycle, from creation through use, no matter what physical form the description takes. The Working Group on Standards for Archival Description has recently defined archival description as "the process of capturing, collating, analyzing, and organizing any information that serves to identify, manage, locate, and interpret the holdings of archival institutions and explain the contexts and records systems from which those holdings were selected." Thus, the uses of archives may be included in their description; reference archivists and users might add information gained in using the records to description of them. "Each time a researcher interacts with a collection, something new is learned about the materials; ideally, even information gleaned during reference activities should be captured and integrated with more formal descriptive compilations."[10]

d. Evolution of Intellectual Access to Non-textual Materials. Description of nontextual materials such as photographs and sound tapes has been less standardized than description of textual records. There are few national tools for locating and describing audiovisual holdings, and local description has been uneven. In most repositories, assistance from knowledgeable reference archivists or photographic specialists is still critical for successful research in nontextual materials.

In the past, many repositories did not apply the principles of provenance and original order to nontextual materials. If available, description was idiosyncratic, consisting of item catalogs or lists. Photographs were often removed from their original locations and filed in self-indexing subject files; they often were not described or cataloged further.

Today, most repositories treat nontextual materials as they treat textual materials, maintaining them in original order if it is usable, describing them in inventories, and indexing them in integrated access tools. The adoption of the MARC VM format (*MA*chine *R*eadable *C*ataloging *V*isual *M*aterials) points toward standardized description and information exchange in integrated automated databases similar to those for archival and manuscript materials.[11]

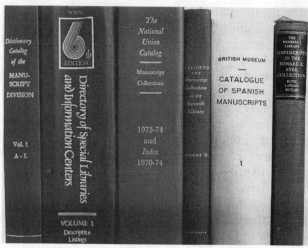

Repositories disseminate information about their holdings beyond the repository in printed guides and directories. (*Sandra Sider, courtesy of the Hispanic Society of America, New York*)

2. Disseminating Information Beyond the Repository

a. Repository Guide. Publishing a comprehensive repository guide was long the ultimate goal of descriptive programs in both archives and manuscript repositories, but automated databases may soon supercede them as the primary means of disseminating information about holdings outside the repository. Although guides can be widely distributed, effective access to them requires that libraries acquire, catalog, and retain them. Guides are soon out of date, and updated editions are usually slow in coming. Furthermore, for guides to be effective, users must know or suspect that a particular repository has material of interest and look for its guide. The NHPRC *Directory* serves as a bibliography of guides if users know of it. In sum, published guides have proven of only limited usefulness in making archival materials known outside the repository, although they are frequently useful to researchers using a particular repository.[12] The recent development of online databases with subject, function, and form access for archives and manuscript collections may change the method for compiling such guides, since databases allow for customized, more frequently printed guides.

b. National Union Catalog of Manuscript Collections. The first reference tool to describe and index manuscript collections from repositories throughout the United States was the *National Union Catalog of Manuscript Collections,* volumes

[10] "Archival Descriptive Standards: Establishing a Process for Their Development and Implementation," *American Archivist* 52 (Fall 1989): 442, 441.

[11] Mary Lynn Ritzenthaler, Gerald J. Munoff, and Margery Long, *Archives and Manuscripts: Administration of Photographic Collections* (Chicago: Society of American Archivists, 1984); Linda J. Evans and Maureen O'Brien Will, *MARC for Visual Materials: A Compendium of Practice* (Chicago: Chicago Historical Society, 1988).

[12] Roy C. Turnbaugh, "Living with a Guide," *American Archivist* 46 (Fall 1983): 449-52.

published annually by the Library of Congress since 1959.[13] Familiarly known as NUCMC ("Nuc Muc"), it briefly describes each manuscript collection reported by participating repositories, and indexes the description by names, places, and subjects. As seen in Figure 3-3, the entry for each collection includes name and life dates of its creator, collection title, inclusive dates, size, and a note about its contents; name of repository; citations to other descriptive tools; and statements on access, copyright, and provenance. As of the 1988-89 volume, NUCMC had published descriptions of 60,565 collections in 1,350 repositories, and indexed them with approximately 682,100 entries for names and subjects.

The success of NUCMC has been uneven. NUCMC relies on the voluntary reporting of manuscript repositories, and many repositories do not participate. Small collections are excluded; more importantly, because institutional, organizational, and governmental archives maintained by the creating institution are excluded, NUCMC omits vast quantities of archival materials. Its quality depends on descriptive information provided by widely varying repositories. Indexes have been cumulated at uneven intervals and are somewhat cumbersome to use. The *Index to Personal Names in the National Union Catalog of Manuscript Collections 1959-1984* by Harriet Ostroff has, however, simplified access to over 200,000 personal and family names in the separate indices. As NUCMC has grown, the multiplicity of volumes, the need to search several indexes, and the difficulty of revising descriptions to accommodate changes in collection content or access have made it increasingly frustrating to use.

From 1959 until 1985, NUCMC was prepared manually. The 1986-1987 volume, which appeared in 1990, was prepared in cooperation with the Research Libraries Information Network (RLIN), an online catalog system maintained by The Research Libraries Group, Inc. Annual printed volumes will continue to be published by the Library of Congress from information maintained in the RLIN database. Repositories that are not part of the Research Libraries Group will report collections manually to NUCMC, and the NUCMC staff will add information about their holdings both to NUCMC and to RLIN.

c. Subject Surveys. Published by scholars or national research organizations, subject surveys also disseminate information about holdings. Such

guides typically describe holdings at the collection or record group level. Well known examples include Richard C. Davis, *North American Forest History: A Guide to Archives and Manuscripts in the United States and Canada* and the massive *Women's History Sources* edited by Andrea Hinding, et al. Manuscripts of notable literary figures are itemized in *American Literary Manuscripts: A Checklist of Holdings in Academic, Historical, Public Libraries, Museums, and Authors' Homes in the United States.*

d. Online Public Access Systems. The role intended for repository and subject guides may now be more successfully played by recently developed online public access systems (OPAC). Using the MARC AMC format, archivists and manuscript curators can disseminate information about holdings to users and archivists through national, regional, or local online bibliographic databases. Automated databases are capable of printing both repository guides and subject guides.

Such databases initially grew out of the economies of shared book cataloging. In the 1960s the Library of Congress developed the MARC format as a standard for exchanging bibliographic data in machine-readable form so that libraries might manipulate it for internal purposes such as cataloging, acquisitions, and circulation. Regional library networks and bibliographic utilities, which serve as central processing facilities for member libraries, quickly developed to exploit the economies of sharing bibliographical data and other cooperative library services. At the simplest level, members locate a bibliographic description in the central database, modify it for local use, and either order it in the form of a catalog card, or download it into a local database. If the item has not been cataloged, the member contributes its cataloging record to the database. The use of these databases for reference use was unanticipated, and bibliographical utilities are only now exploring the uses of information beyond technical services.[14]

Most notable for archivists are the two national bibliographic utilities, OCLC (Online Computer Library Center) and RLIN (Research Libraries Information Network). Both became "national without the benefits of national planning."[15] Both began as

---

[13] An earlier attempt was Philip Hamer, *A Guide to Archives and Manuscripts in the United States* (New Haven: Yale University Press, 1961).

[14] Katharine D. Morton, "The MARC Formats: An Overview," *American Archivist* 49 (Winter 1986): 21-30.

[15] David Bearman, "Archives and Manuscript Control with Bibliographic Utilities: Opportunities and Challenges," *American Archivist* 52 (Winter 1989): 28. See also Joyce Duncan Falk, "OCLC and RLIN: Research Libraries at the Scholar's Fingertips," *Perspectives* 27 (May/June 1989): 15-17.

Figure 3-3 *The National Union Catalog of Manuscript Collections*

MS 64-18

Mountain States Athletic Conference.

Records, 1937-62. 14 ft.

In Brigham Young University Library (Provo, Utah)

Correspondence of conference commissioner E. L. "Dick" Romney, minutes, financial records, conference operating code, statistics, newspaper clippings, and papers on athletic meets and disputes.

Unpublished register in the library.

Deposited by Mr. Romney, 1962.

MS 64-19

Mooney, Thomas Joseph, 1882-1942

Papers, 1906-42. ca. 44,600 items.

In University of California, Bancroft Library (Berkeley)

Labor leader. Correspondence and other papers concerning Mooney's trial and conviction for murder in connection with the bombing at the Preparedness Day parade, San Francisco, July 22, 1916, and efforts to secure his release. Includes trial records, Mooney's prison correspondence; correspondence of the various defense organizations (particularly the Tom Mooney Moulders Defense Committee); correspondence of Governor Culbert L. Olson concerning the pardon; financial records; newspaper clippings (some in scrapbooks); script and film of motion picture; pamphlets, and propaganda material. Early papers include material relating to Mooney's activities with the San Francisco street railway employees union and personal correspondence.

Report and key to arrangement, available in the library.

The Library of the University of California at Los Angeles has carbon typewritten copies of ca. 250 legal documents, correspondence, and other papers (1916-35) concerning Mooney's trial and efforts to obtain a pardon.

MS 64-20

Teague, Charles Collins, 1873-1950.

Papers, 1901-50. 103 boxes.

In University of California, Bancroft Library (Berkeley)

Rancher, of Santa Paula, Calif. Correspondence, reports, speeches, memoranda, bulletins, accounts, photos, and printed material relating primarily to Teague's career as president of various companies and associations connected with the citrus industry in California. Includes papers pertaining to Teague's service with the U. S. Federal Farm Board (1929-31), to the failure of the St. Francis Water Supply Dam (1928-29), and as regent of the University of California.

Report and key to arrangement available in the library.

The Library of the University of California at Los Angeles has positive and negative microfilm copies (30 reels each) of the collection and ca. 1200 duplicates of papers in the collection.

Gift of Harriet (McKevett) Teague and Milton Teague to the University of California at Los Angeles, 1954; the papers were microfilmed in 1959 and the originals sent to the Bancroft Library, University of California at Berkeley.

MS 64-21

Abbott, Edith, 1876-1957.

Papers of Edith and Grace Abbott, 1903-54. 45 ft.

In University of Chicago Library.

Correspondence, notes, documents, pamphlets, bibliography, and other papers (mostly since 1910) relating to the professional and academic careers of Edith Abbott as dean of the University of Chicago School of Social Service Administration, and her sister, Grace Abbott (1878-1939) as chief of the U. S. Children's Bureau. Includes Edith's correspondence (1910-20) when she was a resident at Hull House with Jane Addams, Julia Lathrop, and Florence Kelley (1859-1932). Grace's papers relate chiefly to affairs of the Children's Bureau and to public welfare administration and also concern immigration problems and political opposition to Federal welfare activities. Correspondents include Jane Addams, Margaret Bondfield, Sophonisba P. Breckinridge, Homer Folks, Felix Frankfurter, Florence Kelley, Harold Laski, Julia Lathrop, Katherine Lenroot, Julian Mack, Frances Perkins, Julius Rosenwald, Lillian D. Wald, and others. Organizations represented in the correspondence include the American Association for Labor Legislation, American Association for Economic Freedom, American Association of Social Workers, American Association of University Women, American Child Health Association, American Public Welfare Association, American Social Hygiene Association, Better Homes in America, Boston Settlement Study, California Institute on Social Work, Canadian Council on Child Welfare, Character Education in the Public School, Chicago Probation Project, Chicago Recreation Commission, Child Labor Committee of Illinois, Child Welfare League of America, Children's Bureau, National Civil Service Reform League, Cook County Bureau of Public Welfare, Committee to Clarify the Constitution by Amendment, Emergency Peace Campaign, Encyclopaedia Britannica, Grand Island College, Great Lakes Institute, Hull House, Illinois Conference on Social Welfare, Immigrant's Protective League, International Council of Women, International Penal and Penitentiary Commission, League of Nations, Mobilization for Mount Holyoke College, National Child Labor Committee, National Conference on Outdoor Recreation, National Conference of Social Work, National Consumer's Research League, National Council on Naturalization and Citizenship, National Education Association, National Federation of Business and Professional Women's Clubs, Pan American Child Welfare Congress, Save the Children Foundation, Social Science Research Committee, Spanish Child Welfare Association, Textile Committee of the Fair Labor Standards Act, Twentieth Century Fund, Washington Council of Social Agencies, and Works Progress Administration.

Unpublished guide in the library.

Gift of Arthur G. Abbott, 1957; and University of Chicago Graduate School of Social Service Administration, 1962.

MS 64-22

Aldis, Mary (Reynolds) 1872-

Papers, 1860-1918. ca. 100 items.

In University of Chicago Library.

Poet and lecturer. Notes, clippings, and transcriptions of poems, mostly concerning World War I, taken by Mrs. Aldis from books, magazines, and newspapers for her lecture, War poetry, old and new.

Information on literary rights available in the library.

Gift of Graham Aldis, 1949.

MS 64-23

American Association for the United Nations. *Illinois and Mid-west Office.*

Records, 1936-42. 4 ft.

In University of Chicago Library.

Papers dealing with educational activities of the organization, such as contests and model League of Nations councils and assemblies for high school students; coordinated programs with the Chicago Peace Council and the National Peace Conference; and dissemination of literature concerning neutrality legislation. The association worked chiefly through the World Citizens Association and the Commission to Study the Organization of Peace after the U. S. entered World War II.

Unpublished guide in the library.

Gift of the association through Quincy Wright, president of the Executive Committee of the Mid-west branch, 1955.

The National Union Catalog of Manuscript Collections, 1963-1964 (Washington, D.C.: The Library of Congress, 1965), 57.

databases of information about books, primarily to support cataloging and other technical services, but increasingly both hold information about other cultural resources, including archives and manuscripts. Description in these databases is guided by the conventions of the MARC formats.

Archivists and manuscript curators began to participate in these national databases in the mid 1980s, and the full implications of national databases for archives and manuscripts are only beginning to be realized. Participation in national databases has obvious implications for users and reference archivists, but the use of national databases has conceptual, political, and financial implications for the bibliographical utilities as well.[16] A major concern at this writing is that users must have access to both national systems to be certain of finding all reported sources.

OCLC developed to share cataloging information. Including the holdings of a wide variety of libraries, it supplies cataloging data, holdings information, and interlibrary loan services to its member libraries through a group of regional networks. In 1990, recognizing increasing reference use, OCLC developed the EPIC service to provide subject access and keyword and Boolean searching capabilities to a variety of databases including its own Online Union Catalog. Late in 1991, OCLC announced an extension of those capabilities, the FirstSearch Catalog, which will allow individual researchers to search directly through a menu-oriented interface, rather than relying on reference staff for searches.

Implementation of the MARC AMC format in OCLC is somewhat constrained, for the size of each entry and the number of added names and subjects are limited, and, at this time, it cannot search on function or form index terms. Currently, OCLC is most successfully used to search for known items, or known corporate or individual record creators.

RLIN describes the holdings of some 100 research libraries and archival repositories. It is part of the Research Libraries Group, which was founded in 1974 by large research libraries and went beyond the economies of shared cataloging to share other cooperative services in collection management, acquisitions, preservation, and interlibrary loan. Special memberships allow research institutions like archives and manuscript repositories to join. Many small repositories will contribute to RLIN through NUCMC, and others through incorporation of statewide guide projects.

Use of the database by reference staff and users, initially a secondary benefit, is now recognized as the primary use of the database. In 1989, reflecting this change of emphasis, RLIN began charging for database searches, rather than cataloging uses, and made it possible for individual researchers to use the database, in addition to access by participating repositories. RLIN has extensively implemented the MARC AMC format. RLIN entries may be searched by personal or corporate names, and terms for occupation, subject, function, and form. RLG is participating in projects that explore the use of functional analysis, the use of shared appraisal data (including records schedules), and the use of administrative histories in providing provenance authority information. The RLIN database increasingly is a reference database for information about records creators as well as about records reported to it, as seen in Figure 3-4.[17]

e. National Inventory of Documentary Sources. The *National Inventory of Documentary Sources in the United States* (NIDS) is a microfiche publication of inventories and registers gathered from repositories throughout the United States. Begun in 1983, there are four parts, to be updated periodically: (1) Federal Records, (2) Manuscript Division, Library of Congress, (3) State Archives, Libraries, and Historical Societies, and (4) Academic and Research Libraries and Other Repositories. Each part is accompanied by a bound volume that lists finding aids and provides a name and subject index. This reference tool complements other national finding aid systems such as NUCMC, RLIN, and OCLC, by reproducing the full text of unpublished inventories and registers. NIDS offers users anywhere the opportunity to examine actual unpublished finding aids, most of them hitherto available only in the various repositories. The quality of the publication, however, depends on the voluntary participation of repositories, and its use on its availability in libraries.

Information from Holdings

In most repositories, providing information *about* holdings has traditionally been the primary focus of reference service; in some repositories, however, providing information *from* holdings is an important part of reference service. In the first case, the archivist helps users identify likely sources, and users do their own research, identifying, evaluating,

[16] Bearman, "Archives and Manuscripts Control."

[17] *Using RLIN for Archival Reference* (Mountain View, Cal.: Research Libraries Group, 1991).

Figure 3-4   Government Records in the RLIN Database

What do descriptions of government records in RLIN look like?

Among the government records in RLIN, there are two types of entries: those that describe agencies creating records (agency histories), and those that describe the records these agencies create (records series descriptions).

Agency histories provide information about the origins, development and functions of an agency. Knowing the history of an agency and its functions enables a researcher better to understand the information an agency creates and why that information was created

Records series descriptions provide information about records an agency creates in the course of its functions and activities. Some records series descriptions also show where records are located when they are not in an archives, and may include decisions about the retention or destruction of records along with the archives' reasons for those decisions in terms of their appraisal of the records' value for legal, administrative, historical, evidential and other uses.

Agency History

Oregon. State Board of Control. Agency history record.

The Board of Control was established in 1913 to coordinate the management of state institutions, construction of state buildings, and other duties assigned by the Legislative Assembly. The Board consisted of the Governor, the Secretary of State, the State Treasurer, and an executive secretary. The Board was the governing body for institutions, including the Oregon State Penitentiary; the Oregon State Hospital; Eastern Oregon State Hospital; Fairview Training Center; Tuberculosis hospitals in Salem, The Dalles, and Portland; the Oregon State School for the Deaf. The Board was responsible for overseeing the maintenance and construction of the State capitol, the Capitol Mall, the Portland State Office Building, the Public Services Building, Salem, and several other state buildings. In the 1960's the Board created the Corrections Division; the Mental Health Division; the Special Educational Services Division; and the Research and Program Evaluation Division. The Board of Control was abolished in 1969. Its responsibilities were divided among the Dept. of Human Resources, the Secretary of State, the Governor, State Treasurer, and the State Highway Commission.

Records Series Description

Oregon. State Board of Control. State institution reports, 1935-1966. 7 cu. ft.

Organization: Chronological by month of report.

Summary: Series documents monthly activities of state institutions administered by the State Board of Control. Types of reports include monthly populations statistics; farm, garden, and dairy reports; summary of institution activities; per capita expense reports; land use reports (1940's); and patient program reports.

Location: Oregon State Archives, 1005 Broadway NE, Salem, OR 97310.

Records Series Description with Appraisal and Retention Notes

Massachusetts. Bureau of Municipal Facilities. State program grant files, 1979-[ongoing] ⟨100 cubic ft.⟩

Organization: Arranged by grant program, thereunder by project number.

Summary: To further the mandate of the Department of Environmental Protection, the Bureau of Municipal Facilities was established in 1989 under the department's deputy Commissioner for municipal assistance to administer grants to municipalities for water supply and water pollution projects, previously administered by the Division of Water Pollution Control and the Division of Water Supply. This series was created by those divisions and is maintained by the bureau to administer grants in the form of outright allocations of funds, reimbursement of costs incurred by municipalities, or low-cost loans. Grant files contain applications, correspondence, revisions to grants, engineering reports, approved and executed specifications, contracts, change orders, approved and as-built plans, and closure documents. Files include information about project planning, facility location and features of proposed site, facility design, construction process, equipment and materials used, costs, and funding sources. In some cases, specifications and plans may be stored separately.

Appraisal statement: Files have administrative value until closure. Fiscal information is not audited in this office. Since the approved application is an agreement, records have a legal value that expires at 6 years after closure with the statute of limitations of actions on contracts. The record copy of this series is held by the municipal engineering department, local water district and/or the facility itself, which holds certain of the materials, such as executed specifications and as-built plans, permanently.

Retention and disposition: Retain in office until closure then retain at state records center for 7 years then destroy.

Location: Dept. of Environmental Protection. 1 Winter St. Boston, MA 02108.

Reprinted with permission of The Research Libraries Group, Inc., from *Government Records in the RLIN Database: An Introduction and Guide* (Mountain View, Cal.: Research Libraries Group, 1990), 4.

and synthesizing relevant information from documents. In the second, archivists supply information from their own knowledge, from finding aids or reference tools; in some cases, they conduct research in their holdings to answer questions.

Requests for information *from* holdings rather than *about* them raise the delicate matter of distinguishing between reference service and research, a distinction usually clearer in theory than in practice. As discussed in Chapter 2, some users request factual information; others request interpretation or evaluation of information. Many factual requests are quite simple: supplying a date, locating a photograph, finding a name. In many cases, a straightforward factual question can be answered by relatively simple research requiring little evaluation or interpretation by the archivist. In a college or university archives, for example, supplying the dates of a student's attendance is probably a simple task. In contrast, a request to supply or even identify letters, diaries, and other documents recording attitudes towards fraternities in the 1890s demands research—evaluation and interpretation that are more often the responsibility of the researcher.

The appropriate response to requests for information from holdings depends on institutional mission and staff resources. Many repositories respond to requests for straightforward factual information, but will not undertake extensive or substantive research. A state archives, for example, may locate and copy a Civil War service record if the researcher supplies a soldier's name and unit, but decline to fill in the blanks in a family genealogy.

Providing substantive research services for the parent institution may, however, be a significant responsibility of reference service in institutional archives. As employees of the parent institution, archivists provide research services for it. A corporate archivist notes, "The staff does the research and provides the answer—it may be one word, two hundred pages of photocopies of original documents, or a six-page synopsis of our research findings."[18]

Providing extracted information, rather than direction to relevant records, is likely to become more important for archives. Charles Dollar notes, "As the shift from print to electronic materials becomes more pronounced in the decade of the 1990s, researchers will expect customized electronic services for specific information. In this environment,

a critical issue for archives reference service is how to shift to a demand-driven reference service that accommodates researchers' expectations and need for information, not records per se." If archives are to survive in an increasingly competitive information environment, archives, particularly those in organizational settings, must become service agencies providing information services their primary constituencies need.[19]

Supplying detailed, comprehensive management information for administrative queries makes the corporate memory a living, vital part of the entity and integrates the archives into current organizational decision making. Such an activist role runs counter to the notion of the archivist as the impartial servant of future scholarship, but is more likely to garner the resources for the identification and retention of records of enduring value.[20]

Repositories need policy statements to guide staff responding to requests for information from records. Such statements should indicate the amount of time that can be given to one query and define how precisely the query must be stated. A repository that must limit research services may state, for example, that ten minutes will be spent searching an index for a name, and a maximum of one hour on a more general query. Written procedures and search protocols will help ensure equity of treatment and search accuracy. If requests are numerous, the use of forms or standard responses may speed response time and ensure that all users receive equal treatment. Staff members should always indicate the sources of the information supplied and the extent of the search undertaken. If additional search might be profitable, the user should be informed of the probable duration and result. Some repositories charge fees for research services. These must be precisely defined.

Repositories, especially those with large outside constituencies, also might maintain lists of local individuals who undertake research for others. One source is graduate students at a local university; universities often maintain a job placement service for part-time student workers. Other sources are local

[18] Cynthia Swank, "Life in the Fast Lane: Reference in a Business Archives," *Reference Services in Archives* (New York: Haworth Press, 1986), 82.

[19] Charles M. Dollar, "Archival Theory and Practices and Informatics: Some Considerations," paper delivered at The University of Macerata, Italy, 7 September 1990, 18. Dollar says that archival reference service today is "supply-driven." Archives accession records which they hope researchers will use in person by searching finding aids, identify boxes they hope will meet their needs, and browse through boxes until they find the information or conclude that it is not there.

[20] David Bearman, *Archival Methods* (Pittsburgh: Archives and Museum Informatics, 1989).

genealogical societies, which often can provide lists of volunteers or researchers available for contract work, and national organizations such as the Board for Certification of Genealogists, which also maintain lists of researchers.[21] When furnishing the names of such individuals, the repository should stipulate that these researchers are independent contractors and that the repository cannot guarantee their work.

Information about Records Creators

On closer analysis, many requests for information, especially those received by organizational archives, are actually inquiries about records creators, not requests for information about or from holdings. Information about creating organizations or individuals is useful to agencies and departments inside and outside the creating institution and to individual researchers.

In the course of locating records, analyzing the creator's functions and organizational changes over time, and arranging and describing their records, archivists compile rich historical information about records creators, and organizational functions, activities, events, and precedents. This is generally an unappreciated and untapped information resource. Archivists need to link their information about records creators with the reference needs of other departments in creating organizations, individual researchers, and information professionals.[22]

Some of this information is incorporated in administrative histories and biographical notes in inventories, but it is often helpful to build reference files in addition to the inventory. Compiling information about records creators, especially in institutional archives, makes it possible to respond quickly to questions. Frequently useful are agency or departmental histories, lists of officers or department heads with their dates of tenure, chronologies of organizational name changes, organization charts, genealogies, lists of publications, histories of buildings, biographies of leaders, and chronologies of important dates. Lists of significant "firsts" in organizational history are useful, but in some cases it is wise to have such lists cleared by the legal department, especially if they are to be used in advertising. Such information can be produced in updatable handouts or filed in loose leaf binders for photocopying. Archi-

vists also are beginning to capture information about records creators in automated systems or in authority files, such as the agency histories in the RLIN database.[23]

Reference staff frequently maintain a vertical file of clippings, pamphlets, and brochures about people, departments, events, buildings, and subjects. The results of searches to complex questions can also be filed in such reference files for future use. They may compile binders of copies of frequently requested photographs arranged by topic. If space in the research room permits, a reference set of frequently consulted published documents, such as minutes of the governing authority, yearbooks, annual reports, newsletters, or journals, can expedite providing information about the institution and other records creators. Indexing such publications of record saves much reference time and contributes to use of the archives. Also useful are monographs based on the holdings or relevant to collection strengths.

While such reference tools are useful for quick responses to factual questions, archivists must guard against developing a parallel finding aid system at the reference desk. If reference archivists discover that they are beginning to develop extensive sets of lists and indexes, then analysis of the descriptive program is warranted.

Referrals

If their repositories do not hold needed information or records of interest to researchers, archivists may be able to provide referrals to persons, institutions, libraries, or repositories that do. Through their knowledge of creating organizations or their records management programs, archivists often know which office maintains information in records not yet transferred to the archives. Because archives are the organizational memory of an institution, archivists play an integrative role in linking information sources throughout the organization. Manuscript repositories may play a similar role for documentation created in its collecting area, even if records are not actually held by the repository. Curators often direct researchers to other archives and manuscript repositories with appropriate related materials or to libraries with related published sources.

Most reference archivists develop a Rolodex or other index of names, phone numbers, and addresses of people and institutions to which frequent referrals

---

[21] Board for Certification of Genealogists, 1307 New Hampshire Avenue, N. W., Washington, D. C. 20036.

[22] Bearman and Lytle, "The Power of the Principle of Provenance," 25.

[23] David Bearman, "Authority Control Issues and Prospects," *American Archivist* 52 (Summer 1989): 286-99.

are made. The directories, guides to other repositories, subject surveys, and other published finding aids described above are also useful. As more information about archives is added to local and national databases, such referral networks will become even more useful.

* * *

Providing intellectual access traditionally has meant providing information about repositories and their holdings. In many settings, and increasingly in an information economy, archivists also provide information from records, information about records creators, and referrals to outside information sources. Archivists, as the guardian of memory, can play increasingly important roles in helping users find the information they need.

Archivists use a variety of finding aids, which have evolved and continue to do so, to provide intellectual access to archives and manuscripts. Reference archivists provide a critical link between these finding aids and users seeking information. They educate users about the process of doing research in archives, and help users identify and locate the finding aids, records, and information needed for their research. Because assistance from reference archivists is so often vital to the success of users in archives and manuscript repositories, we will turn in Chapter 4 to an examination of the reference process.

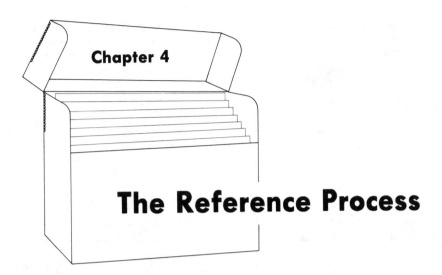

Chapter 4

The Reference Process

Providing reference services is an interactive process that evolves through three phases—initial interview, continuing assistance, and follow-up activities. Because reference archivists frequently mediate among users, finding aids, and records, understanding the interaction among these elements during this process is critical to providing intellectual access to archives. Although in many cases the reference interaction takes place in person, reference services are also provided by phone, mail, and electronic communications systems. Beyond assisting individual users, reference archivists also provide services to groups of users and potential users through public programs. This chapter examines the reference process in each of these circumstances.

Reference Interaction

The extent of reference interaction varies from simple to complex, depending on the nature of the repository, the kinds of finding aids available, the research problem, and users' research skills. Not all users require, or even desire, all elements of the reference process, nor do all repositories provide sufficient staff to carry them out.

Reference interaction has both intellectual and administrative elements and is affected by interpersonal dynamics between user and archivist. The quality of reference service depends on acknowledging and successfully resolving the complicated dynamics of reference transactions. An effective reference interaction enables a user to exploit archival resources fully, while meeting the administrative requirements of the repository.

Intellectual Elements. As an intellectual exchange, reference interaction, also called question negotiation, consists of three activities: query abstraction, resolution, and refinement.[1] Query abstraction and query resolution take place during the initial interview, which usually marks the beginning of reference service, although sometimes letters or phone calls precede it. Since query refinement takes place during research, interaction between user and archivist may be needed throughout the research project. Interaction may be extended by phone or mail follow-up activity after the researcher leaves. In Figure 4-1, the reference process is shown as a "black box" in which the archivist processes an inquiry to produce a list of records relevant to it. Figure 4-2 expands the "black box" to illustrate the steps followed during query abstraction, resolution, and refinement.

1. The Initial Interview. Beginnings are delicate, and the initial interview sets the tone for all that follows. Because clear communication between user and archivist is essential to make best use of holdings, the initial interview often is crucial to a user's experience in an archives. The initial interview facilitates intellectual interchange between archivist and user. It is the archivist's opportunity to elicit information about the research project and to guide the user to the necessary sources. The archivist

---

[1] The best discussion of the intellectual aspects of reference interaction in archives is found in American Management Systems, "Methodology for Developing an Expert System for Information Retrieval at the National Archives and Records Administration" (Washington, D.C.: National Archives and Records Administration, 1986).

Figure 4-1   Modular Software Model

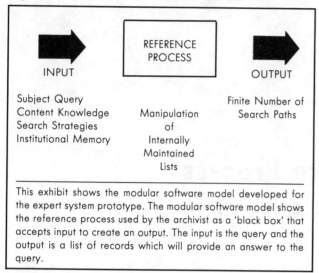

This exhibit shows the modular software model developed for the expert system prototype. The modular software model shows the reference process used by the archivist as a 'black box' that accepts input to create an output. The input is the query and the output is a list of records which will provide an answer to the query.

(Courtesy of American Management Systems)

Figure 4-2   A Model of the Reference Process

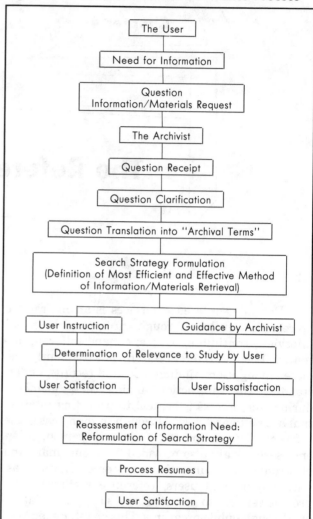

Developed by Sandra Kiemele, Civic Records Archivist at the City of Calgary Archives. Reprinted from *Canadian Library Journal* 47 (October 1990): 356.

ascertains what information the user needs to answer a particular question, and the amount, variety, level, and complexity of the source materials needed to resolve it.

First, in the query abstraction stage of the reference interview, topics are identified and delimited by geographic location and time period. Archivist and user strive to clarify questions and to state the full scope of the research problem. In some cases it is necessary to narrow the user's initial question, in others to broaden it. By asking good questions, the archivist helps the researcher raise all relevant issues. In this stage, the archivist tries to glean enough information to translate the user's natural language into the retrieval language of the finding aid system. Eliciting names of specific persons, organizations, places, and events is important, because research subjects must be linked with the collections and record groups created by specific individuals and organizations.

During query abstraction it is also frequently helpful to learn about the intended uses of the information, for the nature of the intended product may indicate which type of sources will be most useful. Is the researcher writing a dissertation or a term paper, producing a documentary film or videotape, preparing a report for a public policy agency, seeking legal precedent, or satisfying curiosity? It is also useful to find out whether the user is asking on behalf of someone else, as is frequently the case in institutional archives. Because negotiating a question through an intermediary is difficult, it is best, whenever possible, for the archivist to talk directly to the

person with the question. Ascertaining the amount of time that the researcher has available for the research project also helps determine the nature and depth of suitable resources.

Question abstraction is important whether the user or the archivist will conduct the research. In fact, precision in defining user needs may be more important if the archivist is to locate the information, since the archivist, not the user, must evaluate the relevance of sources and information.

In the second, or resolution stage, the archivist and the user analyze the problem in terms of the sources available and form a search strategy, a plan for resolving the question in light of the sources. The archivist assesses available sources, identifies

Figure 4-3 Completed Search Path

SUBJECT: History of Mission Indian Tribe

GEOGRAPHIC LOCATION: California

TIMEFRAME: 1845-1950

TOPIC AND COMPLETED SEARCH PATH:

1.0 Establishment of Reserves

  1.1 Bureau of Indian Affairs

    1.1.1 Letters Received 1824-1881 [jurisdiction]

    1.1.2 Letters Received 1881-1907 [Alphabetical Groupings]

    1.1.3 Letters Sent 1824-1957 [Alpha Grouping-1881-1907]

    1.1.4 Central Classification Series 1907-1957 [Indian Agency; decimal scheme]

  1.2 Bureau of Land Management

    1.2.1 Division K [Indian Reserves]

  1.3 Office of the Secretary of the Interior

    1.3.1 Indian Division

      1.3.1.1 Letters Received 1849-1880

      1.3.1.2 Letters Received 1881-1907 [alpha group]

      1.3.1.3 Letters Sent 1849-1907

2.0 Establishment of Schools

  2.1 Bureau of Indian Affairs

    2.1.1 Letters Received 1824-1881

      2.1.1.1 Index By Jurisdiction

    2.1.2 Letters Received 1881-1907

      2.1.2.1 Index in Alphabetical Groupings

    2.1.3 Letters Sent 1824-1957

(Courtesy of American Management Systems)

records, and suggests an order in which the researcher might use them. Based in part on an assessment of the probability of finding useful information, the archivist helps the user identify some sources as highly relevant, others as possibly useful, and others as of marginal interest. The archivist may answer some factual questions from personal knowledge or ready reference sources. For other questions a published history will be sufficient, and for yet others multiple sources will be needed, including archives, manuscripts, photographs, motion pictures, sound recordings, and electronic data archives. In Figure 4-3 is shown a completed search path, a list of series in the National Archives relevant to a query about the Mission Indian Tribe in California 1845-1950.

The arrangement of a series may dictate research strategy. For example, to use a series arranged by name, the researcher must have the names of individuals; similarly, to use a geographically arranged series effectively, the researcher must know the area of interest. Sometimes, one group of records must be used first in order to learn information necessary to use another.

The archivist's response to the user's query depends in large measure on the level of description and the types of finding aids available. In some cases, the archivist identifies terms for searching catalogs and databases. In others, the archivist identifies likely record groups and series. In still other cases, the archivist locates and explains the use of finding aids likely to guide the user to relevant sources. Increasingly users have identified holdings of possible interest through national or local databases, but they still rely on archivists to explain archival arrangement and the use of inventories and other finding aids. Archivists may also use national reference sources, knowledge of holdings of other repositories, and knowledge of sources retained by creating departments within the parent organization to refer users to relevant information sources outside the repository. The complicated relationships among archivists, finding aids, records, and users in resolving questions are suggested in Figure 4-4.

The resolution stage of question negotiation is particularly important in institutional archives. The archivist translates a question about a subject into a question about the related organizational functions. Knowledge of institutional history is necessary to ascertain which agencies were responsible for those functions in the period under investigation and thus likely to have recorded the needed information. The archivist also uses knowledge of the forms in which information was recorded to infer which records series might bear on the subject, to suggest, for example, that annual reports will be more fruitful than minutes.

A question about a department may lead beyond its own records to an analysis of information flows within the parent organization to locate all relevant information, including that transmitted to other departments. For example, a thorough study of a university's English department may require use of the records of the governing dean, academic vice president, president, faculty senate, and governing board. Further resolution may lead to a printed bibliography of faculty publications and to the database that succeeded it.

In manuscript repositories, a similar process takes place. The reference archivist uses knowledge of the activities of the people and organizations whose papers the repository has collected, knowledge of the kinds of information found in such ge-

Figure 4-4   Use of Shared Knowledge and Reference Data

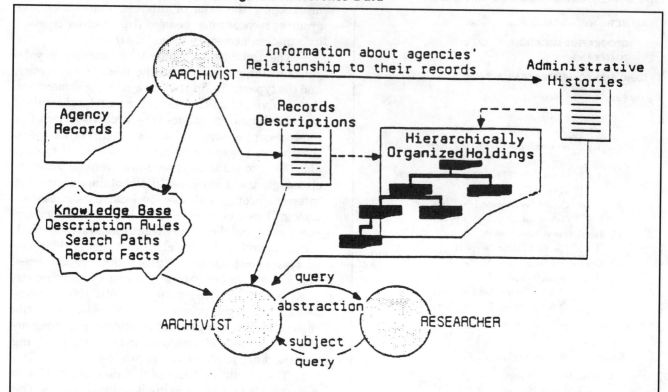

As the exhibit shows, there is a great deal of knowledge shared between the various archivists as they go about the job of managing the Archives' holdings and retrieving information from them. The key finding aids are the *descriptions* and the *administrative histories*.

The descriptions show what records were produced by given agencies. The histories show directly what the agencies missions were, and therefore indirectly what kinds of information they used and produced.

The archivists draw on a knowledge of these items in their work, as well as an institutional memory of rules-of-thumb about how records are described, the best way to search for information in them, facts about record contents, and so on.

(Courtesy of American Management Systems)

neric types of records as diaries or field notes, and knowledge of the repository's finding aids to identify relevant collections. Since manuscript collections do not reflect functions embodied in organizations and recorded in particular record forms to the extent that archives do, the process is necessarily less distinct.

Although the query abstraction and resolution stages of the reference interaction are distinct, they often occur simultaneously. For example, a researcher's interest in a particular organization, such as the Grand Rapids Kindergarten Training School, may lead directly to its inventory to locate appropriate series, boxes, or folders. In contrast, a broad subject request, such as a request for sources for a history of early childhood education, requires more extensive abstraction and resolution. It will lead to a longer

discussion, first, of the terminology used to identify this concept over time and, second, of the individuals and organizations likely to have participated in its development. This negotiation may lead not only to the records of the Grand Rapids Kindergarten Training School, but to the papers of its founder Clara Wheeler and to the records of the Woman's Christian Temperance Union, which promoted legislation to establish public kindergartens.

The reference process in archives is often inferential, based on what is known about the records, their creators, and the circumstances of their creation. This process sometimes gives archivists an "illusion of omniscience" to users unfamiliar with archival research. For example, a user inquired whether a noted Victorian author had ever visited Ann Arbor, Michigan. The archivist suspected that

An archivist helps a user with the MARS—Manuscript and Archives Retrieval System—database. (*Jim Mercer, courtesy of Department of Cultural Resources, Archives, and Records Section, North Carolina*)

the author would have written to University of Michigan President James B. Angell and knew that Angell's correspondence was indexed by name. With this information it was relatively simple to find a letter from the author discussing the date of his visit. Knowledge of the date gave access to local newspapers, university publications, and diaries for descriptions of the visit.

By explaining their reasoning to users, archivists can help researchers build their own research skills. It is important to help users understand records creation, finding aids, and the process leading to a particular search strategy. Archivists strive to make users as independent as possible by helping them to think archivally—that is, functionally and hierarchically. As teachers, archivists help users to think, "Who would have been likely to record the information I am seeking, how would it have been recorded and filed, and where are the records now?"

2. Continuing Interaction during Research. Interaction between archivist and user is often needed after the initial interview to refine the problem and search strategy. This is the third stage of reference interaction. Research in archives is iterative. As users work through archival materials, they discover new aspects of their topic, including the names of other organizations and individuals whose activities bear on the subject of research. These names must be linked with other record groups or collections. Additional discussions, similar to the initial interview, are needed to clarify and resolve these new questions.

Researchers also discover questions about the records as they work through them. These problems of external evidence are very much the archivist's

concern. Provenance-related questions about the source, creation, or custody of records can help the user judge the authenticity of documents, understand bias or interpretation, or explain gaps in the records. Users also may need technical assistance—deciphering hand writing, identifying archaic words or references, resolving problems with dating, or using difficult file structures. Archivists also may help users understand how best to use formats new to them, such as photographs, maps, or electronic records.

Other questions that arise during research concern repository policies and procedures. Simple questions about retrieving or photocopying materials may often be answered by nonprofessional support staff. Substantive or complicated administrative questions—for example, copyright or publication—cannot be delegated, and matters of intellectual substance must engage the attention of professional staff. Support staff must be trained to recognize which questions to refer.

3. Exit Interview. Ideally, reference interaction is closed by an exit interview as long and thorough as the initial interview, but this is seldom realized. Because users do not always announce their departure, it is wise to request and, if possible, schedule an exit interview during the initial interview. Although continuing interaction during research helps to insure that researchers have seen all pertinent materials, an exit interview provides an opportunity to review the sources used and to discover if additional materials warrant another visit. Reference archivists can clarify policies for publication, citation, and the use of copies, and request a copy, or least a citation, of publications or other products based on repository resources.

An exit interview also is an opportunity for users to evaluate repository services. Users can assess finding aids, report on arrangement and preservation, suggest leads for acquisition, and evaluate reference services. An exit interview is not the only way to obtain such information; other follow-up activities will be discussed in Chapter 8.

Interpersonal Dynamics. All phases of reference interaction—initial interview, continuing assistance, and exit interview—are affected by interpersonal dynamics between user and archivist. Although little research has been done on the dynamics of reference interaction in archives, librarians have studied reference encounters extensively, and archivists can learn from this research if they note the significant differences between the two. The most significant difference is that reference encoun-

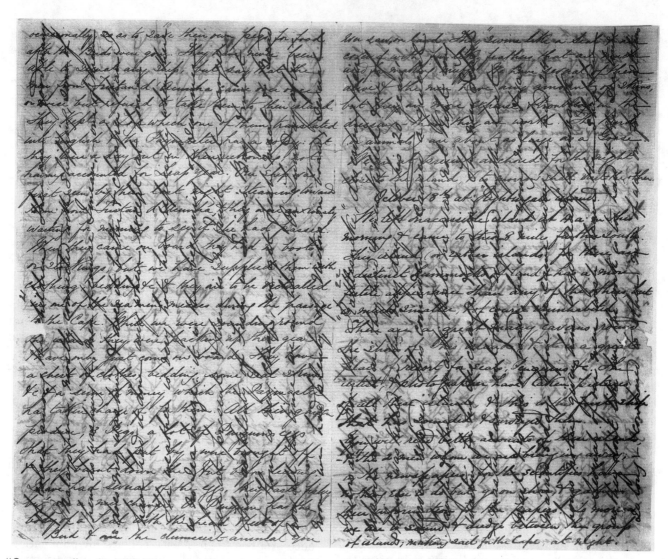

"Cross writing" in this 1873 letter was used to conserve paper and reduce weight of mailed pieces. It makes difficult reading for current researchers. (*Scripps Institution of Oceanography Archives, University of California, San Diego*)

ters in libraries are usually short and voluntary, each devoted to a single question. In contrast, reference transactions in archives are more likely to be substantive, obligatory, and continuing.[2]

Nonverbal signs and symbols are significant components of interpersonal communication. These subtle messages can either reinforce or subvert the overt messages sent or received verbally. Often people are not fully aware of sending and receiving these covert messages. Research on nonverbal communication in libraries indicates that positive body language makes users feel more comfortable approaching a staff member with a question. For example, eye contact, immediate verbal acknowledgement of the user's approach, and feedback signals such as nodding, smiling, and the so-called "eyebrow flash" make users feel their approach will be welcomed. Correspondingly, negative body language—lack of acknowledgement, no change in body position, frowning, pursing the lips, grimacing, sitting with hand over brow, facing a terminal, or writing—discourages users. Physical distance between people is a significant nonverbal symbol; library research indicates that a user will approach a standing person more readily than a seated person. Nonverbal language is culturally determined and culturally bound. Eye contact in excess of cultural norms can be perceived as threatening, while less eye contact than expected can seem evasive or dishonest. The "proper" distance between people varies with cul-

---

[2] The best introduction to this subject for archivists is Linda J. Long, "Question Negotiation in the Archival Setting: The Use of Interpersonal Communication Techniques in the Reference Interview," *American Archivist* 52 (Winter 1989): 40-51.

A smile and eye contact make a user feel welcome. (Jonathan R. Stayer, courtesy of Pennsylvania Historical and Museum Comission)

ture, class, and gender. Most North Americans are uncomfortable when someone stands "too close," and many South Americans are uncomfortable when someone stands "too far away."[3]

Nonverbal interaction goes both ways; archivists get impressions of users too. Nonverbal messages may influence professional roles and actions, and awareness of interpersonal factors can help archivists treat all researchers fairly. Occasionally, an archivist may dislike a user or find a user extremely difficult to assist, yet provide greater attention to another researcher with a more attractive personality. Archivists must guard against making assumptions, based on a user's mannerisms, about the value of research or level of intelligence and skills.

Initial inquiries are especially complicated by interpersonal dynamics. Often the first question a user asks is not the real question or a full statement of need. Users are at a psychological disadvantage when asking questions because they expose need or ignorance to a stranger whose attitude is unknown. In this vulnerable position, users, fearing rebuff or ridicule, may adopt defensive measures. They may ask a simple directional question to see what kind of response is obtained. If users anticipate a particular response, they may frame the question in accordance with expectation. Users anticipating rejection may ask questions defensively. Some users attempt to bully the staff. Such behavior, though understandable, only conceals the real question and prevents users from fully exploiting repository resources.

Some users may not ask questions at all, thinking that the staff is too busy or that their inquiries

are too trivial. Users new to archives do not expect a lengthy interchange; most expect archives to be like libraries with a catalog and shelves to browse. More experienced researchers, particularly scholars, may feel that they should know how to find information themselves and are embarrassed to admit, simply by asking a question, that they do not. Afraid of appearing inept or uninformed, some users try to bluff, to give the impression that they know more than they do. Others feel superior to archivists or lack confidence in them. A scholar may well know more about a subject than the archivist does, but very likely does not know the holdings of the archives or how best to exploit them.

Thus, most users need to be encouraged to state their problem fully, and, in nearly all cases, the first question, whatever it may be, must be expanded. If the archivist fails to probe more thoroughly, the real problem may not be discovered and the user may not find needed information. Or, if the first question is taken at face value and answered, time may wasted, because the user then says, "Yes, but what I really need is. . . ."

The location of the initial interview is important. Does it take place either at a reference desk in the research room or at the researcher's table in sight and sound of other users? Finding it difficult to admit need, expose ignorance, or seek help in public settings, or not wanting to bother other users, many users respond better in a private setting, such as a separate office. Although in many small repositories all user activities must take place in one room, larger repositories should consider having an office for reference interviews. Regardless of the location of the interview, ready access to finding aids is important because they not only provide needed information for the intellectual components of the interview, but can ease awkward interpersonal relations since user and archivist can focus on shared inanimate objects.

Archivists are also at risk of setting up barriers to communication. They may prejudge the value of certain kinds of research or dismiss some users. Like users, they may suffer from tender egos and uncertain status. They may fear exposing their own limited knowledge and or think that they must be authority figures, instant experts in all fields, able to dazzle and astound all comers with their omniscience. Inexperienced archivists in particular, afraid to appear ignorant, too often hasten to answer the ostensible question instead of asking additional questions to get a better sense of the real problem. Listening is as important as talking. Not only do most users enjoy talking about their research, but

---

[3] Joanna Lopez Muñoz, "The Significance of NonVerbal Communications in the Reference Interview," *RQ* 16 (Spring 1977): 220-24.

An archivist assists a small group in a consultation room. (Ronald J. Monfette, courtesy of Schoolcraft College Archives)

questions and silences can also be employed effectively to give users time to think of relevant terms or concepts.

If a good relationship is forged during the initial interview, interpersonal communications are less likely to be a problem in continuing interaction and the exit interview. Since the direction of research cannot be foreseen, the archivist must maintain contact to maximize assistance to the user. Ascertaining the appropriate degree of continuing contact is sometimes difficult. Some users do not want to be interrupted by staff. Others appreciate a timely question asking whether they are finding what they need, because it indicates that the archivist expects continuing interaction. Determining the appropriate moment to intervene is eased if the archivist can observe the user at work.

Some researchers burden the staff by requesting continuing assistance beyond staff resources, in effect asking staff to do their research for them. Dealing with such people is not easy. Appropriate negative body language can help create necessary distance, but sometimes the most dependent are oblivious to subtle cues. The access policy, discussed in the next chapter, should clearly indicate how much assistance staff can be expected to give. Polite but firm explanation of the policy may be necessary.

The quality of reference service can only reflect the resources allocated to it. Responding to user queries takes time and effort. When faced with a difficult user or under pressure of other work, the archivist may be tempted to answer a direct question, despite suspecting that it is not the real question that needs to be answered. Sometimes coping with such indirect questions seems to require too great an

effort. And, unfortunately, all too often, archivists are too busy to engage in a meaningful dialog. Continuing interaction depends on the accessibility and continuity of reference staff and thus on administrative staff allocations.

Administrative Elements. As will be discussed in Chapter 6, researchers usually register, identify themselves, and check their belongings before they begin their research. They must learn procedures for requesting materials and photocopies, read the rules for proper care of archival materials, and understand copyright and citations. These administrative details can consume considerable time and are likely to be distracting. They can hamper a substantive discussion of user needs and repository resources. In some ways they are counter-productive to the primary goal of the interview— eliciting information about users' needs and devising strategies for meeting them. In many repositories, without some care, such administrative details easily prevail over more important intellectual and interpersonal aspects of reference service.[4]

Balancing the intellectual and administrative aspects of reference interaction is difficult but important. Both staff and user will feel frustrated if they have attended to extensive administrative details only to discover that the repository has no materials of interest. Elaborate registration procedures overwhelm a ready reference question that can be answered quickly from staff knowledge or convenient reference tools.

Administrative matters also frequently dominate both continuing interaction and the exit interview. Requesting and retrieving materials, returning and checking them, handling photocopy orders, assuring security, and reshelving are likely to take everyone's attention.

Administrative concerns can complicate interpersonal dynamics, too. If the archivist must enforce security rules, it may be difficult to gain the trust necessary to develop a full dialog about the research topic. Some users, feeling that they are being treated as potential thieves, find it difficult to discuss their needs fully. The archivist can mitigate this conflict in part by explanation and positive body language, but this takes away energy and time from substantive matters. Many of these conflicts are better avoided by careful building design and furniture layout to ease security concerns and by publications to

4 Robert S. Tissing, Jr., "The Orientation Interview in Archival Research," *American Archivist* 47 (Spring 1984): 173-78 focuses almost exclusively on the administrative elements of the initial interview.

An archivist assists a user at a microfilm reader-printer. (*Gary Griffith, courtesy of Louisiana Baptist Convention Archives*)

explain procedures. In larger repositories, delegating administrative procedures and paperwork to a receptionist leaves archivists to concentrate on the substantive intellectual work of the interview.

Telephone and Mail Inquiries

Off-site users direct inquiries to the archives through letters, telephone calls, and, increasingly, electronic mail and facsimile (fax). For some users, such inquiries initiate or continue research conducted in person, but for many users they are the sole means of interacting with the repository.

Archivists encourage users, especially those from afar, to write or call before visiting. This permits archivists to conduct preliminary searches to identify relevant materials, especially new holdings not widely known. Prior communication helps users decide whether a trip is warranted and helps them

better plan their visits. It prevents them coming unannounced only to find that needed materials are unavailable because they are being processed or microfilmed, in storage or at the conservation laboratory. Access to other records may be restricted or have to be arranged in advance of use.

Some mail and telephone inquiries request information about records, but many request information from holdings or about record creators. The repository needs policies to define the amount of staff time to devote to such research and the types of research to be undertaken by staff. A repository also needs policies for responding to phone and mail requests for copies. Most repositories provide copies, for a fee, of a limited number of clearly identified items, but do not provide staff time for broad subject searches or for making judgments about the relevance of particular documents.

Archivists frequently must balance the needs of researchers in the research room against requests by phone and mail. The user who has expended time and effort to visit in person is usually given priority. Phone calls may be returned after researchers in the research room have been served. Callers with complex questions may be asked to put the request in writing. Such a policy, however, may be modified by institutional mission. For example, in an institutional archives, administrators on the telephone may take precedence over other categories of users in the reading room.

The mail transaction includes some elements of the reference dialogue, but the archivist has limited flexibility in negotiation. In a written response it is best first to rephrase the question as a guarantee of shared understanding and then to answer it at an appropriate level or to explain why it is not possible to provide an answer. For example, the repository may hold no materials relevant to the query, or records may be too extensive for the archivist to search. Copies of portions of finding aids can be enclosed if useful. The archivist should clearly indicate sources of all information, and as time permits, identify other possible resources. In some cases, the archivist may need to request additional information to determine the researcher's real needs.

Large repositories monitor correspondence and phone requests to assure that they are answered promptly by the most appropriate staff member. Reference staff screen letters and, if necessary, route them to appropriate staff. A telephone request form,

Figure 4-5   Telephone Request Form

```
Date of call_____ Time of call_____

Name of caller_____

Name of institution/unit caller represents

_____

Phone number of caller_____

    Best time to call?_____

Address for any correspondence_____

_____

_____

Account number for any fees_____

Summary of request:



Services requested:



Date needed_____ Date completed_____

Staff member_____

Notes:
```

as shown in Figure 4-5, collects both information necessary for a reply and information for evaluating repository use. An indexing system for substantive responses can facilitate future reference work. Alternatively, information learned in the course of research can be added to finding aids or to reference files.

The use of word processing systems can increase efficiency in answering correspondence. Certain types of letters can be drafted by paraprofessionals and reviewed by archivists, and letters drafted or approved by archivists can be formatted and sent by secretaries. Using standard paragraphs to convey frequently requested information is helpful. As noted in Chapter 3, requests for information about the repository and its procedures are usually answered by brochures and other prepared handouts. If the archivist finds that some questions are frequently asked, designing appropriate handouts can save considerable staff time.

Phone and mail inquiries can consume a significant part of a repository's reference resources. If the volume of letters and phone calls begins to exceed

the capacity of staff to respond in a timely manner, solutions must be sought. Ideally, additional staff are hired or reassigned to reference service. If this is not possible, it may be necessary to send form letters explaining that off-site reference requests cannot be answered.

Public Programs

Some user needs can be met more effectively through public programs for groups of users than through personal reference interaction. Planning for public programs involves establishing goals and objectives, identifying constituencies and their needs, developing programs to meet those needs, and evaluating the programs' success in meeting them.[5]

Establishing goals and objectives for educational programs is part of the planning process of the repository as a whole. Public programs are not frills, but an integral part of institutional mission. To use resources effectively, public programs must relate to the goals of the repository and the parent institution. Goals and objectives must be realistic. Typical goals include, for example, informing potential users of holdings, encouraging potential users to visit the repository, or teaching current researchers to use the repository and its resources more efficiently.

Most repositories identify particular publics to be served in their mission statement. Sometimes educational programs for records creators are as important as programs for records users. In some cases the holdings of the repository will suggest groups of potential users. User studies and collection analysis also are tools for identifying constituencies. Analysis of use statistics and demographic profiles of user groups may suggest groups that are underserved or underrepresented. Analysis of collections and collection use statistics may identify bodies of records that are not being used and suggest potential users. For example, a state archives may have significant materials on environmental planning, or a religious archives may have significant materials on ethnic groups that are not being used. Natural constituencies are, in the first case, environmental action groups, and the other, scholars or members of particular ethnic groups. If the reference staff is over-

---

[5] A useful introduction to public programs is found in Ann E. Pederson and Gail Farr Casterline, *Archives and Manuscripts: Public Programs* (Chicago: Society of American Archivists, 1982) and Ann E. Pederson, "User Education and Public Relations," *Keeping Archives.* See also Gail Farr Casterline, *Archives and Manuscripts: Exhibits* (Chicago: Society of American Archivists, 1980).

Figure 4-6 Public Programs

Vehicles for user education include:
- lectures by staff or users,
- conferences for records creators, users, archivists, and other information professionals,
- discussion groups for users,
- guides for using particular sources,
- guides outlining research strategies for common queries,
- subject bibliographies,
- workshops on research methods,
- workshops demonstrating filing principles and applying records schedules, and
- videotapes or slide-tape shows demonstrating research methods.

Interpreting holdings for a broader audience might include
- preparing exhibits and exhibit catalogs,
- writing articles and books based on holdings,
- preparing videotapes or slide-tape shows about subjects documented in the holdings, or
- editing and publishing documents.

whelmed by questions about genealogical research, public programs to meet the needs of genealogists are important both to the staff and to the public.

Identifying the needs of the public to be served also is important. Staff and clients alike contribute valuable ideas. Archivists are likely to perceive that the problem is teaching users how to use the finding aid system; research into user needs also may suggest better ways to design finding aid systems. Survey research is one tool for ascertaining needs and opinions; focus groups are another. Once identified, one or more of the needs can be chosen for immediate focus.

After the needs of the target group are identified, specific programs, services, or products must be identified to meet them. The possibilities are almost endless, limited only by the imagination of the archivist and the resources available. Some of them are listed in Figure 4-6. After the program is selected, its objectives must be defined very carefully. "What do we want to accomplish in this program? What do we want to do for the archives? For the target public?" Objectives must be written and transformed into a workplan. All programs take resources, whether of staff, money, or space. Specific activities necessary to carry out goals and objectives must be identified, as well as particular actors and sources of

funds. A budget listing projected expenditures for staff, supplies, travel, equipment, and other resources is needed.

Reference archivists often present orientation sessions to potential users. Some of the objectives of such presentations are:

1. Disseminating information about records. Learning about the makers and keepers of records, particularly how people and organizations create records, helps users understand how recordkeeping practice affects information in records. Some users need to understand differences between primary and secondary sources. Building from common experiences in libraries, archivists can explain how archival methods and materials differ from other information resources, and demonstrate the full variety of sources beyond published sources. Learning to assess internal evidence, external evidence, and bias in records is often useful.

2. Preparing users for effective research. Learning how archival materials are organized and described assists users in understanding how to locate needed records. Understanding the history and diversity of repositories helps to prepare people for research in a variety of repositories. Suggestions for necessary preparation in secondary sources may assist users to make best use of primary holdings. Learning to write letters of inquiry to repositories, understanding the purposes of various types of finding aids, and using databases are other useful skills.

3. Conducting research in the host repository. Users rely on archivists for information about access, copyright, citation, publication, and photocopying. Examples of note taking can be helpful. Rules and regulations for using the particular repository can also be presented. Often archivists assist students by suggesting topics that can be supported by records in the host repository. Many users profit from exercises using specific records relevant to their topics. Exercises might involve reading documents from a variety of sources that relate to the same event to discuss issues such as point of view, bias, and interpretation. Also useful are exercises in deciphering handwriting and understanding dating conventions.

4. Conducting research in archives generally. Such sessions for users who do not plan specific research projects but wish to learn more about research methodology incorporate the objectives listed above but are more general. The National Archives program called "Going to the Source" is a good example.

Archivists use exhibits to educate the public about the mission and functions of archival repositories. (*Illinois State Archives*)

5. Sharing archival methods with other information professionals. Orientation sessions with other information professionals discuss archival methods for organizing, describing, and managing information in archives. A tour may be useful to see the applications of principles discussed in the session.

6. Educating the public about the mission and functions of the archival profession. Orientation sessions may also be requested or organized for cultural groups, alumni associations, potential donors, or the general public. Orientation sessions are one of the many vehicles archivists use to increase public appreciation of archives and manuscript materials, both as artifacts of civilization and as research sources, and to develop public understanding of the role of the profession as a whole and the particular role of the specific repository. Such programs seek to build support, whether records, money, or time. For example, the videotape "Let the Record Show: Practical Uses for Historical Documents" by the

New York State Archives and Records Administration, designed to be shown at orientation sessions, aims to involve the community in the preservation of historical records.

Since the targeted public must be informed about programs and services available, repository planners should devise and implement a plan for publicizing these products, services, or programs. Archivists must identify the media tools used by the targeted public, which may not be traditional archival tools. Press releases, radio or television announcements, community calendars, newsletters, posters, flyers, invitations, and brochures are among the devices used to reach potential users of archival services.

Evaluating how well the service, product, or program meets the identified objectives is essential if it is to be continued or improved. In some cases, participants fill out an evaluation form. Such evaluations should determine not only participant satisfaction, but also the information or skills that were learned. For example, participants in a workshop designed to teach the use of an automated catalog should be asked if they can in fact find needed information in the database. Use of a pre-test and post-test is often helpful to determine what skills have been learned.

* * *

Archivists should strive to make all users, no matter how they approach the archives, whether as individuals or as groups, in person or through mail or phone requests, feel that they have received helpful, courteous assistance, and their fair share of repository resources. Intellectual, interpersonal, and administrative elements of the reference interaction must be balanced to give users the best possible service in the context of repository mission and resources.

Since archival resources are limited, policies are needed to allocate them. Further, because archival and manuscript repositories contain information that is private and confidential, some information cannot be made available immediately. Therefore, the repository must draw up access policies to guide reference services. These will be discussed in the next chapter.

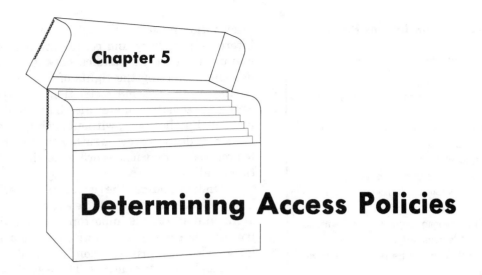

Chapter 5

Determining Access Policies

Access policies reconcile users' need to gain authority to use information with the need to protect some kinds of information from premature disclosure. Reference policies protect records from harm and allocate repository resources for reference services as equitably as possible. Understanding the concepts of privacy, confidentiality, right to know, and equality of access is necessary to determine access policies. Some of these concepts are embodied in law, others in deeds of gift, others in ethical norms. Reference and access are separate issues, yet they are linked in access policies.

Reference and Access

The meaning of the word "access" depends on its context. In a broad sense, as we have seen, it refers to the process of locating needed information, to "the right, opportunity, or means of finding, using, or approaching documents or information."[1] In a narrower more traditional sense, access is "the authority to obtain information from or to perform research in archival records," or "the availability of, or the permission to consult records, archives, or manuscripts."[2] When discussing access, therefore, we must always determine whether we are talking about access broadly defined or in this more limited, legal sense.

[1] Lewis Bellardo and Lynn Lady Bellardo, *A Glossary for Archivists, Manuscript Curators, and Records Managers* (Chicago: Society of American Archivists, 1991).

[2] "Glossary," *Modern Archives Reader* (Washington, D.C.: National Archives, 1984), 339; Frank Evans, et al., "A Basic Glossary for Archivists, Manuscript Curators, and Records Managers," *American Archivist* 37 (July 1974): 415-33.

Although it is customary to discuss reference services and access together and this custom is continued in this manual, determining access policies in the narrow sense is not solely, or even primarily, a reference function. Because reference and access issues have been linked, often inappropriately, they often are confused. As we have seen, reference services and access are associated because reference assistance is critical to obtaining access in the broad intellectual sense. Reference and access also are linked for administrative reasons, since responsibility for administering and explaining access policies to users is a reference function. Also, in most repositories, reference archivists administer physical access to records in the research room.

Most importantly, perhaps, reference and access are linked by tradition. Access to manuscript collections traditionally was granted only to "serious" researchers or scholars, and access to the archives of private organizations was once restricted to members. In these settings, access was a privilege, not a right. Since the archivist decided access questions at the reference desk by examining the credentials of applicants for access, reference and access were linked. In this context access was defined as determining *who* was allowed to use records.

In contrast, repositories of records created by local, state, and federal governments are, and always have been, open to all citizens. Specific information protected by law is closed for limited periods, but, in general, governmental archives and most of their holdings are open to all. In this context, access is defined as determining *when* users are allowed to use *what* information.

Figure 5-1   Archival Responsibilities Regarding Access

Archivists must
- understand laws and regulations relevant to information found in records in the repository, especially federal and state laws governing privacy, confidentiality, and freedom of information, and regulations relating to security classification,
- advise donors and creators about access issues,
- negotiate clear and responsible agreements with private donors and originating agencies,
- know where sensitive information is likely to be found in the types of records acquired,
- identify information that cannot be released immediately for public use,
- develop appropriate restrictions for sensitive information,
- administer restrictions fairly,
- inform users about restricted materials,
- strive to open as much material as possible,
- define a policy codifying access decisions,
- promote equality of access wherever possible, and
- if necessary, advocate legislation or institutional policy that clarifies archival issues in the creation, preservation, access, and use of records.

Today access is, in short, "*Who* gets to see *what* and *when*." The repository must face this issue before users request to use records. Access policies must be determined in consultation with all interested parties, applying relevant laws, in the context of the mission and resources of the repository. When interested users approach the repository, archivists strive to treat them equally. Archival responsibilities regarding access are summarized in Figure 5-1.

Equality of access now governs public use of records in most repositories. Information to be protected is identified and segregated during acquisition and processing. Access policies are therefore administered, but not adjudicated, at the reference desk. Reference archivists must, nevertheless, understand access issues in this narrow legal sense as well as access in the broad intellectual sense so they can administer restrictions and explain them to users.

Access: Concepts and Guidelines. Archivists have a dual responsibility: to the creators and subjects of the records on one hand, and to scholarship and the public good on the other. Archivists seek to make as much information as possible available to users as soon as possible, but recognize that some

information must be withheld to protect legitimate interests of privacy and confidentiality. Archivists maintain a delicate balance between encouraging use and protecting the rights of creators and third parties. Without some restrictions on access to recent and sensitive materials, individuals may be harmed. Furthermore, without such protection, creators may destroy records rather than transfer them to archives, or may not record some kinds of information at all.

Understanding the concepts underlying the laws, regulations, and policies governing access to archival materials is important when designing repository access policies. Four concepts are particularly relevant: privacy, confidentiality, right to know, and equality of access. These guiding concepts are expressed in various forms. The first three are expressed in privacy and freedom of information laws affecting records generated or accumulated by institutions such as federal, state, and local governments, colleges and universities, businesses, and other corporate bodies. Archivists responsible for such records must educate themselves about these laws. All laws affecting records in the institution must be identified, and archivists also must monitor current legislation and modify access policies as needed. Other guidelines regarding privacy and confidentiality are embodied in deeds of gift or transmittal documents and in ethical norms. The following discussion only introduces the concepts and guidelines influencing access to information. Because of the complexities of legal access, consultation with competent legal advisors is often wise.[3]

1. Privacy and Confidentiality. The concept of privacy defines the right of living individuals to be left alone, to keep information about themselves to themselves, and to specify what information they wish to have known. Privacy protects not only good reputation, but also any personal information that individuals want to keep from being known. Some people do not care if their age is known; others feel considerable interest in keeping such information to themselves, perhaps with good reason because they have witnessed or experienced age discrimination. The dead have no privacy rights, a fact important to archivists, since as records age, protecting privacy becomes less a concern.

The concept of confidentiality refers first to private communications. Confidential communication

---

[3] For a fuller discussion of these concepts, see Gary M. Peterson and Trudy Huskamp Peterson, *Archives & Manuscripts: Law* (Chicago: Society of American Archivists, 1985), especially Chapters 3 and 4.

between two people is restricted to them alone, and unauthorized inquiry into the content of the communication is forbidden. Confidentiality is vital to nourishing the trust that enables relationships to function—for example, doctor-patient, lawyer-client, husband-wife, priest-penitent. Some communications are *privileged,* that is, they may be protected by law; neither party can be compelled to testify against the other. Communications resulting from other relationships, such as friendship, may not be protected by law, but archivists may need to recognize and protect the confidentiality implied in them.

Confidentiality also protects private information collected for one purpose from being used for any other purpose during a person's lifetime. Individuals may communicate private information to a person or agency because the law requires it of all citizens or demands it to participate in social programs; in exchange for revealing that private portion of themselves, they are promised that the information will be kept protected from all other uses. People who have entrusted personal information to government agencies, employers, social agencies, or private corporations must feel confident not only that the information will not be used against them, but even that it will not be seen by anyone without legal authority to do so. Examples of records created or accumulated under promise of confidentiality are personnel records, social service case files, disciplinary board files, and investigative files.

The federal government and most states have enacted privacy legislation to protect private and confidential information in governmental records. Privacy acts generally state that the government must tell individuals why personal information is collected and what will happen to it, and declare that personal information will be used only for the stated purpose. Privacy acts generally give individuals the right to see what information has been collected about them, to correct it if necessary, and in some cases to expunge it. Records with personal information usually may be made accessible for research after the death of the individual or after the passage of seventy-five years. The United States Census, which serves as a model for handling personal information, is opened for research seventy-two years after the date of creation.

The Family Educational and Privacy Rights Act of 1974, known as FERPA or the Buckley Amendment, pertains to records of students in educational institutions (20 U.S. Code Annotated 1232g). The law gives the student or the parent of a minor student the right to examine or challenge educational records and prohibits the release of personal information without permission of the student or parent. The law appears to deny all access to educational records with personal information and has been applied retroactively to student records created before its passage. It prompted many colleges to destroy student records rather than transfer them to archives. Many archives have not accessioned student records because of potential access problems, and most have closed student records to research. A few archivists, arguing that scholarly research is allowed under the ten narrow exceptions to the law, have made student records available to users who sign a waiver agreeing not to use or publish personal information; others have deleted names or otherwise screened records. To date, no court test has clarified the legal uses of older student records, but it appears that student records may be opened after seventy-five years.[4]

Issues of privacy and confidentiality also arise in collections of personal papers and in the records of private organizations. In personal collections, there may be correspondence from writers who do not know that their letters have been given to a public repository, or personal information about family members including medical, legal, and psychiatric information of a highly sensitive nature. The commingling of personal and professional lives raises issues of privacy and confidentiality as the distinction between home and office frequently breaks down. Personal papers may contain letters of recommendation, grant application review files, peer review files, and other records about third parties. In the records of private organizations, particularly businesses, there may be internal information regarding proprietary processes, business strategy, or clients that must be protected.

The terms of access to personal papers and organizational records transferred to manuscript repositories are usually spelled out in deeds of gift. The terms of access to institutional records transferred to an archives are usually defined in transmittal documents. A sample deed of gift and transmittal

---

[4] In addition to Peterson, note Mark A. Greene, "Letter to Editor," *American Archivist* 50 (Winter 1987): 3-4; Marjorie Barritt, "The Appraisal of Personally Identifiable Student Records," *American Archivist* 49 (Summer 1986): 263-75; Mark A. Greene, "Developing a Research Access Policy for Student Records: A Case Study at Carleton College," *American Archivist,* 50 (Fall 1987): 570-79; Charles B. Elston, "University Student Records: Research Use, Privacy Rights and the Buckley Law," *Midwestern Archivist* 1 (Spring 1976): 16-32, reprinted in *College and University Archives: Selected Readings* (Chicago: Society of American Archivists, 1979), 68-79.

document and instructions for completing them should be drawn up and reviewed by legal counsel. They should indicate the categories of information to be restricted and identify the length of restrictions.

In general there are two ways to apply restrictions to specific bodies of records: screening users or screening records. The earlier method of protecting information—screening users and admitting to the repository only those persons deemed capable of using information properly—is now discouraged. In the past, repositories often granted access to "serious" users, such as scholars holding the doctorate, but denied it to others deemed less responsible, such as journalists or students. Such restrictions are flawed because there is no guarantee that even the most qualified scholar will not find information that invades privacy or breaches confidentiality. Requiring the donor's permission, another method of screening users, is also flawed. The donor may not be qualified to judge credentials, may not grant access fairly, or may come to resent requests. Donors may be difficult to locate. They age, become ill or senile, and die, often leaving the access question unresolved. Most important, a user who gains a donor's approval may still find information that should be protected. Such donor restrictions should be discouraged, although many repositories find that they must still administer them for older acquisitions.

Some repositories review researchers' notes to be certain they do not contain sensitive information. This too is not a perfect solution for users can remember sensitive information even though they do not note it. Some repositories require that users allow archivists to review manuscripts before submitting them for publication. Such restrictions place the archivist in the role of censor and should be discouraged.

Thus, screening users is frail protection for sensitive information; screening records and closing sensitive portions to research as long as is necessary to protect legitimate needs is far better than relying on the ability of reference archivists or donors to screen users. Screening records before they are made available for research better protects creators and third parties mentioned in the records, and is fairer to users. Access restrictions specified in donor or transfer agreements should describe the precise materials to be closed and the reason for their closure. Restrictions should specify the length of time the records are to be closed, and preferably a date when they will open.

When restricted material is withdrawn from an otherwise open body of records, a withdrawal form left in its place should describe it, the reasons for its removal, and the length of time it will be closed. Withdrawn items should be placed in a secure place and clearly identified so that staff do not mistakenly retrieve them for users and so that they are opened at the expiration of the restriction.

Removing or masking names or other personally identifiable characteristics is another form of screening records; it is particularly useful for case files because they can be made available for aggregate studies without revealing personal information. This method is relatively simple for electronic records, but regardless of format, such information should be removed only from copies of records so that information is not lost.

Reference archivists maintain a list of closed materials and publicize newly opened materials. It is important not to conceal the existence of material, even though it may be restricted or closed. Archivists are obligated to review restricted collections periodically and to open them when possible.

2. Right to Know. Another concept relevant to archivists is the public's right to know. During the French Revolution, the Assembly recognized that citizens must have access to government records to protect themselves and to monitor the actions of public officials. In the twentieth century, however, governments have become more involved in the day-to-day lives of citizens: hence, the question arises, what information held by the government does the public have a right to know?

In a democracy, the public has a right to information about the actions of its government, but people do not have the right to know private information about each other. Thus, the public's right to know must be balanced against privacy and confidentiality. Political scientists, historians, demographers, epidemiologists, geneticists, sociologists, genealogists, biographers, and other researchers request information about individuals or groups to carry out studies that may have profound social implications. Archival access policies and decisions must allow for such research while protecting individual rights.

Freedom of information laws are intended to ensure that records of governmental activities are open to all. The federal statute (5 U. S. Code 552) states that any person has the right to know anything about the operation of the federal government, with nine specifically defined exceptions, including personal privacy and confidentiality. The person requesting information does not have to give a reason for asking for it; but if the agency denies the request, it must show why the information should not be made available. The federal law also specifies time limits to respond to requests. Nearly all states now have freedom of information laws in some form.

In some cases, the public's right to know is limited by the need of the federal government to keep information about some of its actions secure. Such information has been *classified* to prevent disclosure of military or diplomatic information deemed vital to the national security of the United States. The right of the federal government to restrict information about sensitive military and diplomatic activities is recognized, though often controversial and challenged.

Security classification rests on a series of executive orders, and its terms may vary from one presidential administration to the next. Federal officials with responsibility for security-classified documents are not supposed to remove them from federal custody, and records with security-classified information should be found only in federal archives. Manuscript repositories collecting papers of public officials or archives holding records of federal contractors, however, sometimes find security-classified documents. Such materials must be withdrawn from use and secured. The repository must apply to have them declassified, and unless declassified, they cannot be made available to users. The National Archives and Records Administration can help archivists who find security classified information in their holdings to follow proper procedures to protect the records and to secure declassification if possible.[5]

3. Equality of Access. Equality of access to archival materials, another fundamental concept affecting access policies, is an ethical norm of the archival profession embodied in the access statement of the Society of American Archivists. Promoting the broadest possible access for all users on an equal basis, it states that it is the responsibility of a repository "to make available research materials in its possession to researchers on equal terms of access."[6] In general, repositories grant access to all users to all materials, with the exception of those covered by law or other restrictions; in so far as possible, records open to one user are open to all users. Deeds of gift and other transmittal documents should state that materials will be available for research on equal terms of access.

Archivists work to open all materials for research eventually. The SAA policy states, "Repositories are committed to preserving manuscript and archival materials and to making them available for research as soon as possible."Although it may be necessary to close certain bodies of information for reasonable periods to all but the creator, all records will be opened to all researchers at some time.

Equality of access is not always easy to practice. Although archival ethics call for all archives to open as many of their holdings as possible, most archivists serve two constituencies, their employers and the general public. As David Bearman states, institutional archives on the one hand are "clearly a housekeeping function of the organization of which they are a part, and are beholden to that organization for efficient management of an information resource," and on the other hand, serve "a broader cultural master, one who rarely pays the bills and is stingy in its praise."[7] For archivists in institutional archives this dilemma is particularly obvious; institutions often attempt to protect themselves by limiting access by outsiders. Archivists in institutional archives frequently find themselves advocating to the parent institution (and its lawyers) the broader cultural values of archives. Archivists in manuscript repositories founded on a research rationale are today less likely to face pressure for unequal access policies, although the heritage of the great manuscript repositories clearly favors the academic scholar over other user groups.

In addition to advocating equal access for all users, archivists strive to give equal service to all users. Archivists in both archives and manuscript repositories are unlikely, however, to have sufficient resources to be able to serve all users equally and must therefore devise policies to administer access and reference fairly.

Defining Access Policies

A well-considered, written access policy that reconciles equality of access, the right of inquiry, and the rights of privacy and confidentiality is a basic requirement for sound archival management. It should be written as one of the repository's founding documents, adopted by its governing authority, and reviewed regularly. Its provisions must be known to all — staff, donors, and users. Acquisitions staff consult this policy when negotiating with records creators and donors, processing staff when iden-

---

[5] National Archives and Records Administration, Washington, D.C. 20408

[6] "Standards for Access to Research Materials in Archival and Manuscript Repositories," *American Archivist* 37 (January 1974): 153-54. This statement, slightly revised, was jointly promulgated by the American Library Association and SAA. It is reproduced in Appendix 1. It is under revision.

[7] David Bearman, *Archival Methods* (Pittsburgh: Archival and Museum Informatics, 1989), 43.

Figure 5-2   Elements of an Access Policy

1. User Communities. Identify the communities of users to be served by the repository.
2. Resources and Restrictions. State generally the types of records sought by the repository. State the types of information that may need to be restricted. Identify applicable laws and institutional information policies that apply to information in the repository, and append them to the policy. Indicate how restrictions will be applied.
3. Intellectual Access and Reference Services. Describe the finding aids, levels of reference services, and the relationship between the two. If necessary, specify distinctions in service levels. Describe searching services, copying services, and service by phone and mail.
4. Fees. Indicate what services the repository will charge for.
5. Physical Access and Conditions of Use. Describe how records will be made available for research. Include rules for using materials and policy statements for researchers.
6. Use of Information. Establish policies to respond to requests for permission to publish from holdings. Indicate forms for citations. Determine terms for staff use of holdings.
7. Loan of materials. Specify conditions under which materials will be loaned.

tifying and segregating sensitive materials, and reference staff when administering legal access. The access policy, whose elements are outlined in Figure 5-2, also guides priorities for the reference services necessary to provide intellectual and physical access and outlines policies for the use of information taken from the repository.

1. Identifying User Communities. The access policy should state *who* is admitted to use materials in the context of the repository mission, that is, identify the communities of users the repository serves. Governing legislation defines the users of most repositories; for example, the National Archives is open to all. Access to some institutional archives is limited to employees of the parent institution. The institutional mission of other repositories identifies categories of primary users, such as administrators of the parent institution or students of the parent university.

The access policy should state the principle of equality of access, defining user constituencies as broadly as possible and giving access to research materials to all. To the extent possible, repositories

should admit users who do not belong to identified primary constituencies, even though services for them may, in some circumstances, be limited.

No exclusive use of materials should be allowed. In the past, some manuscript repositories granted exclusive rights to use particular collections. In some archives, staff of the parent institution have been granted similar rights. Such exclusionary policies should be discouraged. As the SAA access policy states, "A repository should not deny access to materials to any person or persons, nor grant privileged or exclusive use of materials to any person or persons, nor conceal the existence of any body of material from any researcher unless required to do so by law, donor, or purchase stipulations." If materials are temporarily withdrawn, such as for microfilming or loan, other users must be informed of these special conditions. Archivists also should discourage donors from granting exclusive use to their papers, although the custom of granting access only to authorized biographers is difficult to end. Deeds of gift should not be used to institutionalize unequal access.

Any exceptions to the fundamental principle of equality of access to archival holdings should be spelled out, as appropriate, in the access policy. There are six categories of exceptions. First, the recipient of documents, who is usually the donor, and the creator of documents stand in a special relationship to the material. Repositories may allow access by the person or the staff of the agency that created, received, or assembled the records, while restricting access by others for a reasonable period. For example, staff members from a department of social welfare, in the course of current departmental work, may be granted access to case files closed to outside researchers.

Second, the policy may deny access to anyone who has a claim against the institution. Explicit rules of discovery under the law cover such instances, and archival records may be subpoenaed for use in litigation. The access policy should describe policies for responding to these situations.

Third, minimum age limits are acceptable; it is common to require that students under the age of sixteen be accompanied by an adult. Fourth, the access policy should deny further access to researchers whose demonstrated carelessness or irresponsibility threatens the integrity of holdings. Fifth, the policy should deny physical access to the repository to those not using archival materials. For example, in universities, students frequently seek a quiet place to study; they should be referred elsewhere. Last, the use of original documents may be restricted if facsimiles are made available.

2. Research Resources and Restrictions. An access policy should include a general statement of the types of records available for research and describe the kinds of information that may be restricted by law or donor agreement. Federal and state laws and regulations or information policies of the parent institution applicable to the types of records acquired by the repository should be cited, and the texts appended to the access policy. Likewise, a sample gift agreement or transmittal document and instructions for completing it should be part of the access policy. The policy should spell out in some detail procedures for administering applicable laws and donor agreements. In particular, it should indicate how restricted materials are identified, and the length and review of restrictions. The access policy should specify an appeal process for users who believe they have been unfairly denied access to materials.

Occasionally a user will discover materials that should have been restricted. Since information about taxes, investigative methods, clients, disciplinary actions, proprietary business, or other confidential subjects can appear in unanticipated places, reference archivists should be alert for sensitive information that may not have been adequately screened. Although it may seem unfair to the user, such material must be withdrawn from use. The access policy should outline the procedures for the reference archivist to follow if such circumstances occur.

The access policy also should state clear procedures regarding the use of unprocessed collections. Many repositories limit their use, while others allow access to unprocessed materials if their order and condition allow it. Some records arrive with well-organized file order and detailed lists or indexes. Such materials might be used without staff intervention or with minimal processing. Others arrive in such disarray that they cannot be used before at least preliminary processing. If the archivist suspects that records include sensitive materials, they should not be made available without processing, regardless of their organization when received.

3. Intellectual Access and Reference Services. The access policy should spell out in some detail access in the larger intellectual sense: the relationship of finding aids and the role of reference assistance in locating information. To the extent possible, the repository should strive to make all materials equally accessible to all users through arrangement and description, while realizing that this ideal

will not always be met. As discussed previously, in general archivists assist users in locating relevant records, but in some circumstances archivists also conduct research for them.

Archival resources are limited, and it is a rare repository that has sufficient resources to provide all services requested by all users. Although striving to treat all users equally, archivists recognize that equal access does not necessarily mean equal service. That is, equal access in the narrow sense (authority to use materials) does not necessarily mean equal access in the larger sense (assistance in locating or using information). Some repositories, because of their mission, find it necessary to provide greater levels of service to their primary constituencies. In other cases, limited resources may limit services.

Necessary limitations and priorities must be acknowledged in the access policy. The definition of services available to each constituency will depend on the repository's institutional mission, the nature and size of its holdings, and the available resources of staff, space, and equipment. The type of staff assistance available should be spelled out, by category of user if appropriate. Distinctions in service levels should be articulated. The level of service that can be provided by telephone and mail also should be identified. If resources are limited, specific time limits should be prescribed. The policy also should set forth the kinds of copying services available, fees charged, and time required to process orders.

4. Fees. The access policy should explain all fees related to the use of materials. Since making materials available for research is a fundamental archival responsibility, charging fees for access to the repository or for using research materials in the repository is discouraged, although fees for services such as photocopying or extended searches are customary.[8] Publicly supported repositories should not charge fees for access or for providing information about holdings; some state archives, however, charge fees for out-of-state mail requests for information from holdings. Some private historical societies require that researchers become members of the society, usually at a nominal level.

Occasionally, when copyrights held by a repository have significant monetary or symbolic value, the repository must decide whether it will charge publication fees for commercial use of its materials. Many repositories charge publication fees for com-

---

[8] "Statement on User Fees and Access," *SAA Newsletter* (Jan. 1974).

mercial use of photographs, but few charge for publication of manuscripts.

5. Physical Access and Conditions of Use. The access policy should specify the physical conditions under which research materials may be used. Archivists have an important responsibility to protect the integrity of their holdings. Rules governing the use of materials must be written, distributed to all users, and equitably enforced. They will be discussed in greater detail in Chapter 6. Permissible methods of notetaking and procedures for requesting copying also should be specified.

If a repository's resources for providing physical access are inadequate to meet the demands of its potential users, it faces difficult decisions. For example, what is done if all seats in the research room are taken and another user arrives? How can the repository balance its responsibility to make materials available while also protecting the integrity of the materials? Materials needing less security such as microfilm or publications may be used in an auxiliary reading room, but what should be done after all satisfactory compromises have been exhausted? If a repository is likely to face such circumstances, its access policy should indicate the circumstances in which the archivist is justified in turning users away and establish priorities for determining who will be denied access. Will access to the reading room be on a first-come, first-served basis, or will some users, such as staff of the parent institution take precedence? Will time limits be placed on use of microfilm readers or other equipment? Will all users be required to make appointments? While such decisions may need to be made in emergency situations, such constraints on research should not be allowed to continue indefinitely. The repository must seek resources of space and staff to meet demands for physical access.

6. Use of Information. The use of information taken from the holdings also should be explained in the access policy. As will be discussed in Chapter 7, provisions of copyright law that apply to the repository and its holdings must be identified and policies for copying and publishing from the holdings specified.

Publication. Responding to requests for permission to publish is often a reference function. Answering such queries is greatly eased if ownership of copyright has been determined during acquisition and stated in the deed of gift and in finding aids. If a donor has assigned copyright to the public, any user may publish freely from the material. Although many repositories ask donors to transfer their copyright to the repository, copyright is frequently held by the author or the author's heirs. If so, the archivist must instruct users to seek permission from the copyright owner. To the extent possible, archivists assist in identifying and locating copyright owners, often by supplying information from donor files.

Repositories need procedures for answering requests to publish from holdings for which they hold copyright. The repository may handle requests to publish short quotations routinely, granting nonexclusive permission if the quotation is properly cited. Requests to publish entire works require more detailed consideration. For example, manuscript repositories may hold copyright for diaries, journals, autobiographies, or collections of letters that are attractive candidates for publication. In most cases, the repository will not profit monetarily from publication, but making materials more accessible through publication will redound to the credit of the repository. The access policy should specify whether the repository will give exclusive publication rights for such items. If so, will it grant such requests on a first-come, first-served basis, or will it require conditions be met to ensure an editorially sound and attractive publication? Procedures spelling out the obligations of all parties should be explained in the policy. If an exclusive right to publish is given, a time limit should be written into the agreement so that publication rights to the materials are not tied up for an indefinite period.

Citation. Users need guidelines for adequate citations, and the access policy should specify them. Clear and accurate citations are required for good scholarship and facilitate administration of reference services because scholars frequently use footnotes in others' publications to guide their own research work. In the access policy and in procedural statements for users, the repository should indicate the elements necessary to identify items in its holdings; illustrative examples are helpful. In general, citations should identify the item (including, as appropriate, author, recipient, title, date, page number), all filing levels necessary to find it (file, series, subgroup, record group or collection), and the repository. (See Figure 5-3)

Archivists often must educate users to provide full citations for photographs and other nontextual records as well as for written sources. Few scholars cite photographs, for example, with the same detail as for textual materials, perhaps because they regard photographs as decoration or illustration rather than source material. For some publications, such as a newspaper story, a credit line giving the

Figure 5-3

Suggestions for Citing Records in the National Archives of the United States

The National Archives and Records Service is frequently asked to provide recommendations regarding information to be included in footnotes or other references to records among its holdings. The following suggestions should serve this purpose and their use will also enable our staff more readily to locate records that have been cited.

Sequence of Elements in Citation

The most convenient citation for archives is one similar to that used for personal papers and other historical manuscripts. Full identification of most unpublished material usually requires giving the title and date of the item, series title (if applicable), name of the collection, and the name of the depository. Except for placing the cited item first, there is no general agreement on the sequence of the remaining elements in the citation. Publishers, professional journals, and graduate faculties all prescribe their own style. Whatever sequence is adopted, however, should be used consistently throughout the same work.

Full Identification of Archival Material

Because of the greater complexity and more formal structure of archival material, additional elements may be needed in citations not only to fully identify an item, but also to indicate its relative location within a given

record group. The record group is a unit of control for records based upon their administrative origin, and, for citation purpose, is comparable to a collection or an organized body of personal papers. The elements that may be necessary for full identification of archival material, depending upon its complexity, include:

(Item)
    Charles G. Hewett to Aubrey Williams, December 28, 1936,
(File Unit)
    File "Adm. Reports, October thru December 30," Maine,
(Series Title)
    Administrative Reports Received from N.Y.A. State Officers, 1935-38,
(Subgroups)
    Records of the Deputy Executive Director and Deputy Administrator, Office of the Administrator,
(Record Group Title and Number)
    Records of the National Youth Administration, Record Group 119,
(Depository)
    National Archives Building.

In the above example, all of the elements before record group title and number indicate how the agency received or created and where it filed the record.

Guide to the National Archives of the United States (Washington, D.C.: National Archives, 1974), 761.

repository name may be adequate. A full citation—including, as appropriate, collection, series, folder, and image or negative number—is preferable, however, especially because publication of a photograph frequently results in additional requests for it. By fully citing photographs in repository publications, archivists set a good example for other users.

Use by Repository Staff. The access policy should discuss access and use by archival staff. In the course of their work, archivists may discover private or confidential information or have access to restricted materials. Staff must not use or reveal such privileged information. Archivists may not give anyone special access to such information, including themselves, other staff, or researchers.

In the course of their work, archivists also learn about users' research plans. This information is confidential. Archivists should not disclose users' research strategies nor the sources they consulted.

Both the SAA statement on access and the SAA code of ethics suggest, however, that archivists endeavor to inform users of parallel research in the same materials.[9] If the individuals agree, archivists may arrange introductions. As will be discussed in Chapter 6, the simplest way to do so is to request on the registration form a researcher's permission to share such information.

An ethical question arises when archivists learn new information about their own holdings from discoveries of researchers, such as the identification of authorship of an important work or the discovery of hitherto unknown writings of an important writer. To what extent does sharing such information expropriate the intellectual property of the researcher? There are no easy answers to this ques-

---

[9] "A Code of Ethics for Archivists," *American Archivist* 43 (Summer 1980): 414-18. The code is currently under revision.

tion, but it should be remembered that both archivists and scholars are engaged in furthering scholarship and are committed to equal access to materials. In general, such information should be incorporated into finding aids.

While research in records generally enhances archivists' knowledge of holdings and enables them better to serve users or publicize holdings, in some situations archivists conducting research in their own holdings face a conflict of interest in their ability to assist other users. For example, they may be tempted to withhold information from users to protect their own publication plans. The SAA code of ethics recommends handling this potential conflict of interest by clarifying and publicizing the role of archivist as researcher. That archivists are engaged in such research should be made known to other researchers. Archivists should clearly understand their access and publication rights and not overstep these rights.

7. Loan of Materials. In general archival materials do not leave the repository. Occasionally, circumstances allow exceptions to this rule. The conditions under which materials will be loaned, which are discussed at greater length in Chapter 7, also should be specified in the access policy.

* * *

Thus, access policies are necessary to sound administration of reference services. Policies for access in its larger intellectual sense and its narrower legal sense must be in place before users actually examine records and obtain information from them. Archivists strive to provide equality of access to repository holdings, although they find they often must educate both records creators and records users about appropriate access to sensitive information. Access policies rest in part on laws relating to privacy, confidentiality, and freedom of information, and on contracts found in deeds of gift and transmittal documents. Sensitive information should be identified and segregated during acquisition and processing, so that the reference archivist does not have to judge the motives or wisdom of researchers.

Archivists also try to provide equal services to all researchers, but in some settings limitations on services must be acknowledged. Policies and procedures help the archivist to balance user needs against the staff resources available to meet them while also protecting archival holdings from harm.

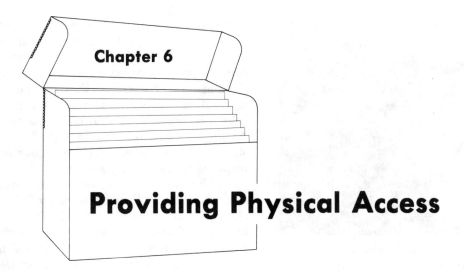

Chapter 6

Providing Physical Access

After identifying records of potential interest and determining that they are available for research, users usually want to examine them. From the repository's point of view, providing physical access necessitates determining policies and procedures for using materials. They must be decided before users are given the opportunity to ask to use records and should be codified in the access policy and explained in a procedures manual so that staff treat all users fairly and equitably.

Use policies aim for a balance between protecting the materials and providing the best service for users. Since the evidential value of archives depends on preserving their integrity, proven through an unbroken line of responsible custody, and since information in archival documents is often unique, records must be protected from tampering and from accidental or thoughtless damage. Records need physical protection from all types of hazards. Although the following discussion considers only the dangers of irresponsible use, archives need facilities that protect records from environmental threats such as fires, floods, and other natural catastrophes. Repositories also extend the life of records by creating a stable environment.

Security

Because repositories must protect records, security is a basic function for all staff. Use policies are the responsibility of reference staff. Secure storage and thorough description of records are two other components of a sound security program. Storage space should be inaccessible from the outside

and also from users of the facility. Because archivists seldom describe individual documents, archival descriptive systems compound security problems and make proving loss difficult or impossible. Traditionally manuscript curators counted documents before and after use, or numbered individual items, but the size of modern collections generally precludes such precautions.

Understanding the motives of thieves and vandals helps archivists to protect documents. Monetary profit is the most obvious motive for theft. Similar but less obvious is the desire to own an important document; some simply seek the joy of possession. Some items in archival custody carry important symbolic value, and even items with little monetary value may arouse personal interest. Some users, particularly those working under tight deadlines, may rationalize theft as a convenient, short-term loan. Surprised to find restrictions on loans or copying, they may fully intend to return the item later. Thus, any document may be a potential candidate for theft, and it is not enough to protect only those of monetary value.[1]

Deliberate destruction and altering of evidence are perhaps greater threats since there is even less chance of recovering from these actions than from theft. People disturbed by an institution's actions may react by damaging its archival holdings because they are an accessible, value-laden part of the insti-

---

[1] Philip Mason, "Archival Security: New Solutions to an Old Problem," *American Archivist* 38 (October 1975): 477-92; Timothy Walch, *Archives and Manuscripts: Security* (Chicago: Society of American Archivists, 1977).

Many book cradles hold large volumes in a state archives research room. (*Department of Cultural Resources, Archives and Records Section, North Carolina*)

tution. Employees may attack their institution in insidious ways by destroying or defacing documents, particularly those of monetary or symbolic value. Similarly, participants in an event or advocates of a cause may wish to purge or alter evidence in contemporary records, to leave the "correct" view of events, to change perceived errors, or to damage someone's credibility.

The integrity of records also may be threatened by careless use, especially if items are left out of order. Provenance and original order are critical both to locating documents and to evaluating their information. If order is disturbed, either by accident or design, documents may be "lost" or evidence distorted.

Repositories have different security needs, and each must evaluate its needs in light of its holdings, descriptive systems, physical facilities, staff, and use policies. It is important to establish procedures to protect records from misuse from both users and staff. Archival staff, who have greater access to documents than other users, may pose the greatest risk. All staff must receive training and ongoing review in archival security. As discussed below, archivists must plan procedures that allow users to read and study documents and devise sensible plans that provide an acceptable and prudent level of care. Use policies and procedures should be developed in the course of repository planning and documented in policy statements and procedures manuals. (See Figure 6-1)

Every archives also needs a plan for responding to suspected theft or abuse and for apprehending suspects without endangering staff, other users, or documents. Archivists often work with local law en-

forcement personnel when devising procedures for apprehending suspected thieves or vandals. If a suspect is caught, archivists should prosecute in the courts. Some repositories shrink from prosecuting or publicizing thefts because they fear negative publicity. Failure to prosecute simply rewards thieves, trivializes serious abuse, and abdicates responsibility. Archivists must work to have thefts, abuse, or destruction of archives taken seriously and to have meaningful penalties assessed.

All but a few users value and respect archival materials. In emphasizing security, it is easy for archivists to lose sight of the needs of users in a thicket of rules and suspicion. It is vital that archivists' concern for the protection of materials not make users feel like thieves and vandals. A welcome smile and cordial greeting must accompany instructions about security provisions. Most users respond sympathetically to security regulations when they understand the reasons for them.

Preservation

Records also need protection to minimize the wear and tear inherent in handling, copying, loaning, and exhibiting them. Ultraviolet light from sunlight and fluorescent lights weakens and embrittles paper. Light also causes fading, and light from photocopy machines is particularly intense. Acid, sweat, and dirt from hands attack the cellulose fibers of paper and photographic emulsions. Physical stress also threatens records. Forcing bindings open, pulling volumes from shelves by the headbands, unfurling tightly rolled maps, or even opening a heavy scrapbook may cause paper to break or glue to separate. Removing items from envelopes and folders may scratch or abrade them if care is not exercised.

Educating users and staff about such problems is vital. Any devices or supplies that can alleviate or prevent such problems should be readily available in the research room. Heavy volumes may need support of book cradles or reading stands. Anyone using photographs should wear lintless gloves to protect images from fingerprints. Making use copies of fragile or heavily used materials can help preserve them and promote use of the information in them. Staff should provide a model for users in handling archival materials, remembering that in the press of daily work, they may be the most careless users of all.[2]

Preservation and reference are further integrated when the reference staff assesses the physical

    [2] Mary Lynn Ritzenthaler, *Preserving Archives and Manuscripts* (Chicago: Society of American Archivists, forthcoming).

Figure 6-1   Repository Security Checklist

_____ Is there a repository security officer?

_____ Is there a procedure to check all applicants' backgrounds before hiring?

_____ Is the repository insured against theft by employees?

_____ Is access to stack and storage areas on a need-to-go basis?

_____ How many employees have master keys and combinations to vaults and other restricted areas?

_____ Is an employee assigned to the reading room at all times?

_____ Do employees recognize the seriousness of the theft problem and the need for vigilance in the reading room?

_____ Have employees been instructed in the techniques of observation?

_____ Have employees been told what to do if they witness a theft?

_____ Has contact been made with the crime prevention unit of the appropriate law enforcement agency?

_____ What type of personal identification is required of patrons?

_____ Are patrons interviewed and oriented to collections prior to use of collections?

_____ Has there been an effort to appraise patrons of the need for better security?

_____ What are patrons allowed to bring into the reading room?

_____ Is a secure place provided for those items not allowed in the reading room?

_____ Do call slips include the signature of patrons? What other information is included? How long are call slips retained?

_____ How much material are patrons allowed to have at any one time?

_____ Are archival materials stacked on trucks near the patrons' seats or kept near the reference desk?

_____ Has the reading room been arranged so that all patrons can be seen from the reference desk?

_____ Do patrons have access to stack areas?

_____ Are patrons allowed to use unprocessed collections?

_____ Are patrons' belongings searched when they leave the reading room?

_____ Do accession records provide sufficient detail to identify missing materials?

_____ Are archival materials monetarily appraised as part of routine processing?

_____ Are particularly valuable items placed in individual folders?

_____ Are manuscripts marked as part of routine processing?

_____ Do finding aids provide sufficient detail to identify missing materials?

_____ Does the insurance policy cover the loss of individual manuscript items?

_____ Does the insurance policy reflect the current market value of the collections?

_____ What is the procedure for the return of archival materials to the shelves? Are folders and boxes checked before they are replaced?

_____ Are document exhibit cases wired to the alarm system?

_____ Are all exterior doors absolutely necessary?

_____ Are there grills or screens on ground floor windows?

_____ Are doors and windows wired to a security alarm? If located in a library or building with easy access, does the repository have special locks and alarms to prevent illegal entry?

_____ Is a security guard needed to patrol the repository after closing?

_____ Are fire and alarm switch boxes always locked?

_____ Are security alarms always secured, tamper-proof, and away from the mainstream of traffic?

_____ Does the repository have a vault or very secure storage area?

_____ Is a master key system necessary?

_____ Does the repository have special key signs to prevent addition, removal, or duplication of keys?

_____ Is after-hours security lighting necessary?

_____ Does the repository have a sprinkler system or other suitable fire suppression system?

_____ Does the repository have adequate fire extinguishers in accessible locations?

_____ Does the repository have a low temperature alarm in event of heat failure to prevent frozen pipes?

_____ Are manuscripts and records stored in areas near water pipes or subject to flooding?

_____ Does the repository have written procedures for fire alarms, drills, and evacuation?

Timothy Walch, _Archives and Manuscripts: Security_ (Chicago: Society of American Archivists, 1977), 30.

Figure 6-2   Decision Tree for Preservation Actions

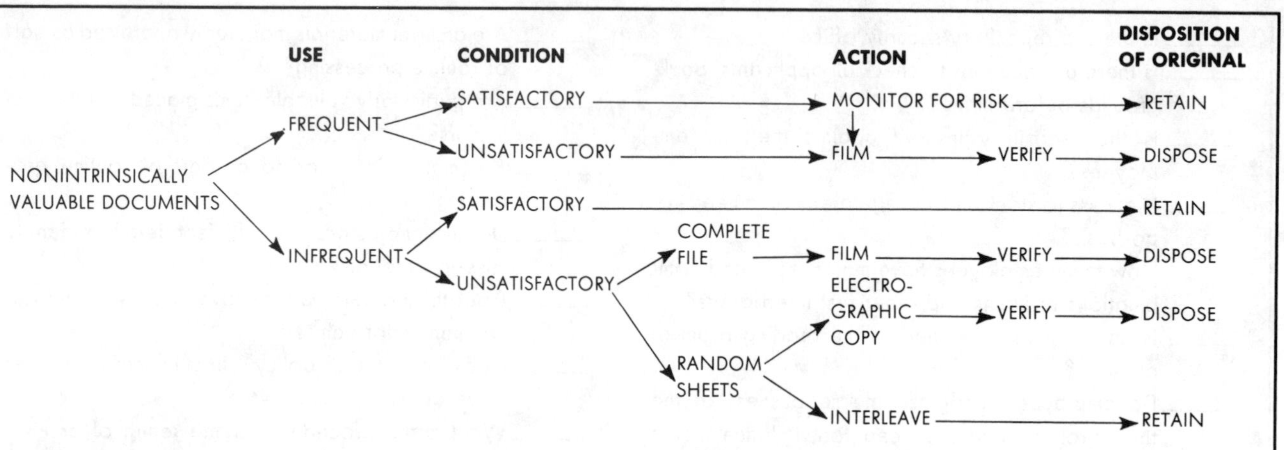

This decision tree marks the places in the process of preserving nonintrinsically valuable documents at which distinctions must be drawn among types of documents or decisions made on treatment. All decisions relate to files only, except in the case of "unsatisfactory random sheets," where a further distinction is drawn on the basis of the ease and appropriateness of photocopying. Verification of copying is always to the degree specified by an archivist for the particular case.

Preservation of Historical Records (Washington, D.C.: National Academy Press, 1986), 87.

status of documents as they are used. Such a point-of-use preservation survey may be a reasonable alternative to a systematic survey of all holdings, since the most heavily used materials may be among the most valuable and vulnerable of the holdings. That is, frequency of use indicates a probable high information value, and repeated use threatens physical well-being. Keeping statistics of use and examining materials when they are used provide a basis for planning conservation treatments, especially preservation copying. The preservation plan of the National Archives, displayed in Figure 6-2, for example, includes a decision-tree for assessing conservation needs based on archival judgments of frequency of use, physical state, and suitability for reproduction.[3] Disaster planning should consider materials in use in the research room as well as material in storage.

Reference Facilities

Security and preservation are two central concerns in planning reference facilities, but the convenience and comfort of users and staff are also important. The research room (variously called the reading room or the search room) should be easily accessible from the outside, and separate from spaces

used to process and store archival materials. If it is not possible to have two separate rooms, the reference desk can provide a barrier between the public and staff areas of the archives. Access for the handicapped is usually specified in building codes. A well-designed research room is quiet, comfortable, and well lighted. Ultraviolet filters on all fluorescent lights help protect documents. A northern exposure, which allows natural light but no direct sunlight, is ideal. If the room has other exposures, shades, ultraviolet filters, or curtains will be needed to control sunlight.

To help users find the parent institution and the repository within it, it is useful to have maps and printed information about parking or public transportation that can be sent to potential users. Information about housing is helpful for out-of-town users. Access is also enhanced by a well-publicized phone number, signs, and other directional devices. Well-designed and attractive signs and brochures make users feel welcome and save staff time. All staff should be able to give clear instructions to users who call for directions, whatever their means of transportation. A telephone answering machine offers small repositories the ability to provide information about hours and services and to take messages even when they cannot answer the phone.

The reference work station should be located close to the reading room, if not in it, so that users have ready access to knowledgeable and helpful staff. Reference staff need a desk or work table

---

[3] Committee on Preservation of Historical Records, National Materials Advisory Board, Commission on Engineering and Technical Systems, National Research Council, *Preservation of Historical Records* (Washington, D. C.: National Academy Press, 1986), 87. This implies that reference archivists need to be trained to recognize preservation problems.

A researcher protects photographs by wearing gloves and supporting images with two hands. (*Nancy Blankenhorn, courtesy of New Jersey Historical Society*)

The guides and inventories of a research center are freely available to users. (*Chris Gratzel, courtesy of Rockefeller Archive Center, North Tareytown, New York*)

equipped with a telephone and a typewriter or, preferably a personal computer or terminal. Staff should have easy access to a photocopier, finding aids, and databases describing archival materials. Ideally, to reduce noise in the reading room, an adjacent room is available for interviews, database searches, consultations, and telephone reference calls. Such an office should allow visual surveillance of the reading room and easy communication with users.

All portions of the reading room must be under staff supervision at all times. It is best if two staff members are on duty so that one, stationed where users entering and leaving the room must pass, remains in the reading room while the other retrieves requested materials. In small repositories, the archivist may have to work in the same area as users during public hours in order to provide such supervision. Tables offer better visual surveillance than desks. A few repositories use closed-circuit television to monitor users. Others mark volumes with "tattle-tapes" that sound an alarm when removed from a designated area without being desensitized, but such measures are not, of course, practical for loose pages.

Users should have the freest possible access to finding aids in or near the reading room without staff intervention, since the purpose of finding aids is to make the user as free of the archivist as possible. Although the SAA statement on access urges that finding aids be made available to users, not all repositories do this. The need to ensure security of finding aids is no justification for denying researchers access to them; security copies of finding aids stored off-site provide adequate protection against fire, flood, theft, or abuse. Unique indexes compiled by records cre-

ators may be treated as part of the record group and users required to sign for them.

A selection of general reference tools appropriate to the subject matter of the holdings also should be available to users in the research room. Such tools as dictionaries, directories, biographies, bibliographies, gazetteers, almanacs, handbooks, manuals, and a perpetual calendar readily at hand will save time for researcher and archivist alike. Institutional archives also might have available reference copies of minutes, annual reports, yearbooks, directories, organization charts, and other reference sources discussed in Chapter 3.

Furnishings and equipment are needed to use the variety of materials held by the repository. Large tables are suitable for maps, blueprints, and drawings; tables with tilt tops or cradles are best for large bound volumes such as newspapers, tax rolls, censuses, and financial records. Book trucks or carts are

Figure 6-3   Equipment for Research Use

Equipment that may be needed to use archival
   materials:
Reader for 16 mm and 35 mm microfilm
Microfiche reader
Reader-printer to make copies from microfilm
   and microfiche
Light table for viewing transparencies,
   negatives, slides
Projection equipment for 8 mm and 16 mm
   motion picture film
Turntables to play 33 rpm, 45 rpm, 78 rpm
   recording discs
Tape recorder for reel-to-reel tapes
Cassette player for audiocassettes
Videotape or video cassette players
Computer terminal for electronic records

needed to transport boxes and volumes. Sand-filled
cloth snakes are helpful to hold open pages of tightly
bound volumes without breaking the spine. It is also
helpful to provide a supply of pencils, a pencil sharp-
ener, and a magnifying glass. Many record forms
require special equipment for use: for example, microfilm, microfiche, motion picture film, sound recordings, and electronic records.[4] (See Figure 6-3.) If
the repository does not own the necessary equipment, it should locate reliable and well-maintained
machines and make arrangements for researchers
to use materials under supervision elsewhere. If
equipment to use early forms, such as turntables for
glass radio recordings, is unavailable, it is best to
copy such holdings onto currently usable formats.
Given the temperamental nature of sound recordings and motion picture films, it is best to have
copies for reference use.

Instructions for use of each type of equipment
should be posted neatly and prominently on or near
the machine. Trained staff should be available to
manage audiovisual equipment and to load and un-
load original materials. If the record button on tape
players is disabled, sound tapes cannot be acciden-
tally erased. Regular inspection, cleaning, and main-
tainance according to manufacturers' instructions
will keep equipment working and reduce damage to
materials.

---

[4] For reviews of equipment, see *Library Technology Reports*
(Chicago: American Library Association).

Policies for Use

1. Hours of Operation. Every repository
should have regular hours of operation, posted prominently and published in brochures and other handouts. It is common to open a repository to researchers
one-half hour after the staff arrives and to close one-
half hour before the staff leaves. Opening only by
appointment may be necessary but is difficult for
both archivist and users. In a one-person archives,
where other duties must be accommodated, regular
hours of operation, albeit limited, allow both archivist and users to plan the best use of time.

Repositories committed to serving a full range
of users maintain evening and weekend hours. Some
repositories staff such hours only with para-
professionals, while others limit reference or retrieval services during the extended hours and require users to arrange in advance so that needed
materials are available. Another solution is to offer
Saturday hours, but close to the public one weekday,
often Monday.

2. Registration and Identification of Users.
Registration and identification of users are customary means to enhance security of documents and to
help ensure that all users have been informed about
rules, copyright provisions, and other such legal concerns. Most repositories require users to show picture identification and acknowledge the rules for
using materials.

Registration forms also enable the archivist to
elicit information about topics and intended use of
information. Such information helps the archivist

A researcher registers at a reference desk. (*Simon Tong, courtesy of
University Archives, SUNY, Buffalo*)

give better service, provides the basis for analyzing how well the repository meets the needs of its users, and documents the nature and amount of use. Archivists also use registration information to build constituencies: to reach users for follow-up evaluations and to inform them of new materials, additional services, or public programs.

Depending on its physical facilities, a repository may need different levels of user registration and identification. Many repositories have exhibits, a museum, a microfilm reading room, or a reference library, which require less security since users do not handle unique materials; these people may be asked simply to sign a visitors log with their name and address so that the repository can count the number of visitors and their sources. If visitors enter the reading room for archival and manuscript materials, they may have to complete more extensive registration.

The more detailed the registration process, the more it becomes a barrier to users. Repositories must balance their need for registration and the user's need to begin work. Before beginning an elaborate registration and interview, it may be useful to conduct a brief initial conversation to ascertain whether the repository is likely to contain materials to meet the user's needs. It is sometimes helpful to separate the purely administrative elements of registration and identification from the reference interview, both to save the time of the reference archivist and to separate reference assistance from security. All staff, however, must be trained to respond warmly and appropriately to all visitors.

Registration Forms. Registration forms, as seen in the sample in Figure 6-4, typically incorporate the following elements:

a. Name, permanent address, and phone number; local address and phone number if visiting.

b. Notation of at least one form of identification, preferably with a photograph, such as a driver's license.

c. Institutional affiliation, and status or occupation. Repositories that limit access to certain categories of users require this information. Other repositories collect it to aid in evaluation and planning. Lists of the most common types of affiliation and of status or occupation, each with an ''other'' category, can be provided with check-off boxes to facilitate entering and collating information.

d. A brief statement of research topic.

e. Statement of intended use of research. The most common products (book, article, dissertation, thesis, term paper, speech, genealogy, film, video-

tape, or exhibit) can be listed with check-off boxes, and space left to write in others.

f. Statement of how the user learned of the repository. Although optional, this element is valuable for evaluating the usefulness of external finding aids and outreach activities. Check-off boxes can list the most common descriptive tools—such as published guide, NUCMC, RLIN, OCLC, library catalog, or brochure—and the most common referral sources—such as teachers or librarians.

g. Application for admission. Whether the user is asked to apply for admission depends on the access policy of the repository.

h. Acknowledgement of the rules for using materials. Users sign the registration form to acknowledge that they have received and read a statement of the procedures for using documents, and that they agree to follow them.

i. Statement regarding use of research information. Users indicate whether archivists may share the general nature of their research with other researchers working in the same subject area. Some repositories also ask whether they may inform others of materials used and request permission to contact the user by phone or mail for future user studies.

j. Name of staff member and date of registration.

Daily Log. Daily use is also often recorded. Most commonly, in addition to initial registration of users, all visitors sign a daily log when they come in; some logs also have space to record the departure time. Other repositories record each daily visit on the registration form. A signed and dated record of visitors in their own handwriting is an important security tool. Beyond security, a record of daily use documents weekly, monthly, or seasonal patterns of reference demand and is useful for planning staffing and services.

Frequency of Registration. Frequency and evidence of registration are handled in several ways. Registration for each research topic gives a more detailed and accurate picture of use, but it is time-consuming for users who return frequently with new topics and projects. Registering each user for a period of time is less time-consuming, though less informative. Registration at least once a year is useful for verifying addresses and reminding users of the rules as well as compiling annual report data. Some repositories issue a reader card that must be presented each time the user comes to do research; others check the registration card on file and issue a daily permit each day that the user signs in.

Figure 6-4   Sample Registration Form

I apply to use the Archives.

Name _____   Date _____

Permanent Address (Street, City, State, Zip)   Permanent phone no.

_____

Local Address (Street, City, State, Zip)   Local phone no.

_____

Researcher Affiliation and Status (Choose one)

1. Parent Institution   2. University/College   3. General   4. Personal
a. Department   a. Name   a. Employer   a. Genealogy

_____   _____   _____   _____

b. Title   b. Position   b. Title   b. Other
                         __ Faculty
_____   __ Staff   _____   _____
                         __ Graduate Student
                         __ Undergraduate
                         c. Department

                         _____

Statement of Research Topic

Intended Use of Research (Check all that apply)

__ Book   __ Article   __ Dissertation   __ Thesis
__ Term paper   __ Speech   __ Genealogy   __ Film
__ Radio report __ TV report   __ Government research __ Exhibit
__ Videotape   __ Personal interest __ Professional research __ Slide-tape
Other _____

Use of Information about You

May we tell others of the subject of your research? __ yes   __ no
May we tell others which materials you used? __ yes __ no
May we contact you by mail or phone as part of future user studies? __ yes __ no

How did you learn about this repository? (Check most important)

__ References or citations in published books   __ Television, radio, newspaper
   Published guides to archives, bibliographies   __ Brochure
      __ Guide to this repository   __ NUCMC   __ Presentation by archives staff
   Databases: __ RLIN __ OCLC __ Local   __ Visit to museum exhibition
__ Teacher, professor, or colleague   __ General knowledge, assumptions
__ Archivist or librarian elsewhere
__ Information from historical, professional, or genealogical organizations
Other _____

Before your first visit on this project, did you write or telephone to get information about holdings or services?
__ yes   __ no   __ don't know

I have read the Rules for Use of Materials and agree to abide by them.

Signed _____

Identification _____   Archivist _____

Figure 6-5 Policy Statements and Forms for Users

- ▼ Location and Hours
- ▼ Access
- ▼ Accommodations
- ▼ Directions (by car, public transportation)
- ▼ Parking
- ▼ Registration and Security
- ▼ Finding Aids
- ▼ Requesting Materials
- ▼ Use of Materials
- ▼ Copyright
- ▼ Ordering Copies (policies, instructions, prices, and forms for each)
  - Electrostatic Copies
  - Photographic Copies
  - Microfilm Copies
  - Audiovisual Copies

A user places belongings in a locker before beginning research. (*Richard Strauss, courtesy of Smithsonian Institution Archives*)

3. Policy Statements for Users. At registration the repository distributes policy statements about the use of documents. It is frequently useful to present not only the rules for using materials, but also additional information that users will need, such as procedures for using finding aids, requesting documents or copies, or citing documents. (See Figure 6-5.) An attractive set of policy statements conveys such information, clarifies expectations, saves staff time, and insures that all users receive the same procedural information. It is unrealistic, however, to expect most users to read and digest a large document before they begin work. To what extent does a large amount of information overwhelm users and hinder good communication, and to what extent does it codify and simplify communication? The balance depends on the researcher, the institutional mission, and the resources available.

Policy statements for users may be issued in a single document, or in individual handouts focusing on specific topics to be distributed as needed. The basic document should include information on the hours of operation, access policy, registration procedures, materials allowed in the reading room, and rules for using materials. To assist users in locating and requesting records, another handout can describe the finding aids and reference services available, give instructions for filling out request forms, state limits on amounts of material that can be requested at one time, and explain procedures for hold-ing materials for future use. A third handout might discuss procedures for requesting copies, explain copyright law and procedures for requesting permission to publish, and suggest forms of citation.

4. Limiting Personal Materials. Limiting personal materials in the reading room is an important security measure to protect documents from being concealed and removed in briefcases, books, handbags, coats, or other belongings. Most repositories allow only note cards and pencils in the reading room; a few supply note paper and pencils for researchers to use. Although repository policy limits what is brought into the reading room, some users do need to bring in reference materials in order to collate materials or to compare information from various sources. Some researchers prefer to use notebooks, which may be quite bulky, rather than note cards. Such exceptions should be authorized only for good cause and decided on a case-by-case basis. It is helpful to list any materials a researcher is allowed

Researchers are now taking notes with portable computers. (*New York State Archives and Records Administration*)

A page marks the place of a box with a withdrawal placard. (*Chuck Scheer, courtesy of Special Collections Department, Boise State University Library*)

to take into the reading room so that they can be checked out at the reference desk when the researcher is leaving. Most repositories examine all materials removed from the reading room.

Ideally there are lockers or cabinets where researchers store personal belongings and a room or rack for coats and outer wear. Commercially available coin-operated lockers can be set so that the coin is returned to users when belongings are retrieved. A table or shelf near the lockers is an added convenience for users as they remove belongings from lockers. If lockers are not available, a locked cabinet behind the reference desk may suffice, but this solution does not give the sense of privacy and control many users desire when leaving handbags or other personal belongings; it also increases the archivist's work and exposes the staff to accusations of theft. The least satisfactory alternative is a table for belongings in view of users and staff.

Users take information from records in many ways. A significant number want to use typewriters or portable computers to take notes; others wish to use tape recorders; still others, cameras. A few users have begun to use optical scanners to digitize information from printed or typescript materials. Most repositories allow typewriters and tape recorders if they can be used without disturbing other users; computers are less disruptive. Noise absorbing pads or shields can be used to muffle the sound of typewriters. Cases that house typewriters or computers should be stored outside the reading room and inspected after the machines are packed before the user leaves. A few repositories supply typewriters or computers for users. The use of cameras is usually restricted in accordance with rules for photocopying, which will be discussed in the next chapter.

5. Requesting and Retrieving Materials. All users, including staff, should fill out and sign request forms, often called call slips or pull slips, for materials that they want to use. Likewise, staff should fill out request forms when they withdraw material for copying, preservation, filming, loan, or exhibition. These forms fulfill several needs and must be designed carefully to meet them effectively. Signed request forms identify material to be retrieved and establish a user's responsibility for it. They also are used to control movement of material in and out of the stacks. Data from request forms can be used to identify heavily used materials, assess acquisition policies and arrangement and description programs, and contribute to decisions about shelving, preservation, microfilming, publication, or outreach priorities.

Carbonless call slips that create multiple copies are particularly helpful. One copy is kept at the reference desk, filed by name of researcher or number of the table or cart on which the material is kept while in use, so that all material issued to a researcher is readily identifiable. A second copy is left in place of the withdrawn item. Some repositories use a third copy that is kept with materials in use or given to users for their record of use. Staff should initial and date all copies when retrieving and reshelving materials.

Once a request form has been filled out, a staff member checks that the user has signed and dated it and that enough information is included to identify the materials to be retrieved. When material is retrieved, a withdrawal flag with a copy of the request form is left in its place; this enables other staff to know where the material is and also helps reshelv-

Researchers are requested to examine one folder from one box at a time. Additional boxes are waiting on a book truck alongside the table. (*Nancy Blankenhorn, courtesy of New Jersey Historical Society*)

ing in order. A large, brightly colored cardboard square with a pocket for the request forms is a useful withdrawal flag.

After the materials have been reshelved, one copy of the form may be filed by name of collection or its control number, and the other by name of user. If a third copy is retained, it can be filed by date. Thus, request forms grouped by collection can be employed to track down problems with holdings, and to answer questions about who used materials and when. Call slips grouped by researcher name can help users identify and cite collections and help staff track collections used by problem patrons.

To prevent accidental mixing of materials, most repositories limit the amount of material delivered to a researcher at one time and further limit the amount in actual use. In general, researchers are asked to use only one folder or volume at a time. Deciding how much material to deliver to a user at one time can be a problem—one folder, one volume, one box, or one cart? For most repositories issuing one box at a time works well; but if sufficient space is available for each user to have a cart parked next to a table, more can be delivered on the cart even though the user has only one box open on the table.

In setting limits, the archivist again balances the needs of users against the needs of the records and the capacity of the staff. Very low limits, such as issuing one folder at a time, slow research and require considerable staff time for many small retrievals and refiles; very large amounts make visual surveillance difficult and increase the danger of misfiling or misuse. To a large extent the limits depend on the nature of the materials. It is unreasonable

to apply the same rules to modern organizational records as to thirteenth-century manuscripts. Both records and users have different needs.

The quantity that may be made available also depends on the precision of the finding aids and the nature of the research problem. In some cases the user and archivist can pinpoint the exact folder or item needed; in other cases the user must examine a large number of items, folders, or boxes to find needed documents or information. Some users, engaged in negative searches to determine that certain documents or information do not exist, may scan a large amount of material in a short time. Other users, tracing a particular statistic or name through a long time series, may move quickly from volume to volume or box to box.

Users who leave materials even for a short time should return all materials to the proper box and close all volumes and containers. When leaving the research room researchers should inform staff what is to be done with materials charged to them. Materials on hold for users returning later is best separated from materials in use and materials to be reshelved, and request forms and other control documents so marked.

When a user has finished with material, staff return it to the stacks promptly, initialing and dating the request forms. To the extent possible, staff inspect the material before and after use. As materials are reshelved, staff can keep a running tally of the number of boxes, volumes, folders, reels, or other units used. Such statistics, if regularly maintained, are useful when planning staff assignments and responsibilities.

How long should a repository keep request forms? In general, the longer the better. The primary reason for long-term retention is security; archivists may not discover theft or abuse for some time. Request slips require storage space, and their filing is time-consuming. If request slips are not organized, however, the value of retaining them is drastically reduced.

6. General Rules for Handling Materials. Rules for use of materials are tailored to the needs of the holdings, but there are prudent standards of care common to the profession. Both researchers and staff must be taught to handle materials with care. All should be instructed to use only one box at a time, to take only one folder from a box at a time, and to handle documents only by the edges while providing enough support from underneath. Users should be instructed not to make marks on documents, trace them or rest an arm or notepaper on the materials. Smoking, eating, drinking, and the use of ink are prohibited. Many repositories provide brightly colored cardboard markers to mark the place where a folder has been removed from a box. Users should be asked to keep materials in their current order and to call apparent misfilings to the attention of the staff. If staff move a misfiled item to another location, they should replace it with a withdrawal form to indicate the new location in case previous users cite it in the former location.

Rules for use of materials should be posted prominently in the research room or on cards on research tables. Instructions for handling fragile or nontextual materials might also be printed and distributed with these materials. Such instructions would indicate how to turn pages of large or brittle volumes, how to remove a photographic enclosure from the photograph, or how to support a photograph.

Automation of Registration and Retrieval Procedures

Archival registration and retrieval systems are ideal for automation. Since standard information is collected from each user, updated frequently, and aggregated for periodic reports, collecting data in an online database promises savings of staff time and enhanced use of user data. Database management software systems can be adapted to collect and manipulate such data. Initially staff may have to enter data, but software systems could be adapted so that users enter information themselves. Eventually, archivists might combine such a registration system with an interactive software package that informs users about the facilities, services, and procedures of the repository, or such software might be coupled with an expert system, such as the prototype developed by the National Archives to identify records of interest to a particular user.

Request forms and other elements of the retrieval system could also be automated. After materials are identified in the repository database, request slips could be printed as needed. Repositories also are beginning to use bar codes to identify and locate boxes or other storage units.[5]

---

[5] For description of an online patron registration system at the Pennsylvania State Archives, see Kathleen D. Roe, "Software News," *MARAC Newsletter*, XVII/3:12-13. Florida State Archives has developed a patron registration system linked to its collection management system. It collects data about users, prints call slips, describes holdings, and provides reports for security and use analysis.

Archivists envision an integrated descriptive system that would include information about use of holdings as well as bibliographic information and information for collection management. As users and archivists discover new information in holdings, it could be added to enrich the database.

Reference Policies for Electronic Records

Making electronic records available for research differs in some significant ways from providing for research in more traditional textual records. Electronic records can be copied quickly, and copies are identical to the original. Electronic records can be also be transmitted off-site without disrupting the original. Therefore, originals are not made available for use. The customary rules for preserving and using textual records are not needed, but other questions arise.

Electronic records have been available for research for several decades now. Initially, most users manipulated and analyzed data sets on time-sharing mainframe computers. Most repositories provided users with a copy of the data on tape and a copy of the documentation describing the data. Most charged for the cost of the tape, or provided copies of the tape to members of research networks. Some, however, also provided programming assistance and statistical analysis. One of the best known of the organizations collecting and distributing machine-readable data to members is the Interuniversity Consortium for Political and Social Research, headquartered in Ann Arbor, Michigan.

New advances in computer technology will change the nature of reference service for electronic records. Thomas Brown of the National Archives suggests that reference services should provide information about or from records where it is wanted, when it is wanted, and in the format in which it is wanted.[6] As archives become part of online networks themselves, users may be able to tap directly into electronic databases managed by the archives, though not necessarily held by it.

* * *

Providing physical access to archives and manuscripts means negotiating a balance between

---

[6] "Standards for MRR Reference Service," *Archival Informatics Newsletter* 2 (Summer 1988): 33-35. See also Margaret Hedstrom, *Archives and Manuscripts: Machine-Readable Records* (Chicago: Society of American Archivists, 1984).

the needs of users, records, and staff. Planning for security and preservation must be integrated with planning services to meet users' needs. Providing physical access primarily means setting administrative policies, but these policies have important consequences for the ability of users to perform their work efficiently. An important part of providing physical access is providing copies and loans. When users begin to use materials, they often request copies of them. Responding to requests for copies and loans is a significant part of reference service and is the subject of the next chapter.

Chapter 7

Copies and Loans

To use information found in archives, users note it, copy it, or borrow the documents in which it is found. They request copies for research use, legal use, publication, and exhibition. Archivists also copy to preserve information in fragile or deteriorating documents. Electrostatic copying, microfilming, and photographic copying are most common in archival settings. Copyright law informs most decisions about copying archival documents, but repository policies and procedures are needed to administer copying services. Although most archival materials do not circulate, loans are occasionally made for exhibition and research use.

Copying

Copying for Research. Many archivists remember when researchers took notes by hand or typewriter. But since note taking is slow, tiring, and prone to error, researchers eagerly embraced technologies to ease it. Microfilming and photostatic reproduction, developed in the 1930s, had a small impact on research patterns because these processes are expensive and require skilled technicians to make copies. Microfilm also requires a reading machine. In contrast, the advent of electrostatic copying in the 1960s, which made inexpensive facsimile copies, revolutionized both office recordkeeping and research in archives. Facsimile copies guarantee accuracy in transcription and allow users to consult the original text repeatedly at their convenience.[1]

With copying readily available, many users do not even bring note cards or paper to the research room; some do not read and extract information from documents at the repository. They photocopy any document that appears relevant for later reading and reference. Users also want materials to be made available off-premises and frequently request copies by phone and mail. Users expect to be able to make not only copies of textual materials but of sound recordings, photographs, motion picture film, and videotape. A few researchers request machine-readable copies of electronic records, a trend that will surely increase.

Copying for Publication and Exhibition. Users also request reproductions for publication, distribution, or exhibition. Reproductions of graphic materials illustrate articles and books and also are disseminated in slide-tape shows, videotapes, television and film documentaries, exhibitions, microform publications, popular magazines, and brochures. Copies of historic photographs decorate restaurants, airports, and other public places. Repositories themselves may profit from selling high-quality copies, suitable for framing, of particularly attractive items such as the first panoramic photograph of a town or the charter of the parent institution. Although many users request 8″ x 10″ glossy black and white photographic prints, others request color transparencies, slides, microfilm, videotape, motion picture film, audio tapes, or oversize photographic copies, increasing the complexity of demands on archival copying services.

Copying for Legal Use. Occasionally archivists are required to produce copies for legal evi-

---

[1] For more detailed treatment of all aspects of reprography in archives, consult Carolyn Hoover Sung, *Archives and Manuscripts: Reprography* (Chicago: Society of American Archivists, 1982).

dence. For copies to be acceptable by a court, archivists must certify the copies of documents from their repositories. Unlike authentication, in which the archivist attests that the document is what it purports to be, certification of a copy is simply a statement that it is a true copy of the document.[2]

Copying for Preservation. Copying materials is also an important preservation measure. For repositories unable to undertake a systematic preservation survey, a user's copying request may provide the first occasion to examine closely the physical condition of an item. If it is so fragile that copying threatens its safety, future use also may endanger it. An appropriate means of copying, usually microfilming, will meet the needs of both user and repository.

If all or part of a collection or series is heavily used and photocopies are frequently requested, the repository might consider microfilming it in its entirety and making copies available for purchase or inter-library loan. The guidelines for determining policies for copying adopted by the Society of American Archivists encourage "orderly microfilming of archives and entire manuscript collections, together with appropriate guides" to improve access as well as to assure preservation.[3]

Preservation copying must meet the highest technical standards. Microfilming should meet legal standards for admissibility as evidence, scholarly standards for use, and physical standards for permanence. The American National Standards Institute (ANSI) has established standards for the technical quality of microfilm, photographic, and electrostatic copying technologies. The National Historical Publications and Records Commission (NHPRC) has established scholarly standards for microfilm projects.[4]

Types of Copies

Commonly requested types of copies include electrostatic, microfilm, photostatic, and photographic copies. If archives hold nontextual record

An exhibit informs users of available copying services for photographic holdings. Another case describes copying services for textual records. (*Courtesy Nebraska State Historical Society*)

forms, they will likely receive requests to copy them as well.

Researchers who want copies in lieu of note taking most commonly request electrostatic copies because they can be made inexpensively and quickly, read without equipment, marked up, and easily collated with other materials. Electrostatic copying is most suitable for unbound documents selected from various parts of a collection or from several collections; it is not recommended for many bound volumes.[5]

Microfilming is a photographic process in which a negative copy is first made, and from which additional negative and positive copies are then produced. It is useful for research, preservation, and publication. Paper copies can be made from an entire roll of microfilm through the Copyflo process, and individual frames can be copied on a reader-printer. Microfilming selected documents from one or more collections for one user is not recommended since the selection will seldom be of use to other users. At some point, if many documents are to be copied from

[2] Gary M. Peterson and Trudy Huskamp Peterson, *Archives & Manuscripts: Law* (Chicago: Society of American Archivists, 1985), 89-90.

[3] "Statement on the Reproduction of Manuscripts and Archives for Reference Use," *American Archivist* 39 (July 1976): 411; now under revision. Reproduced in Appendix 2.

[4] Standards for microfilm are usefully summarized in Nancy Gwinn, *Preservation Microfilming: A Guide for Librarians and Archivists* (Chicago: American Library Association, 1987). Another summary of standards in all areas of reprography is found in National Research Council, *Preservation of Historical Records* (Washington: National Academy Press, 1986).

[5] A useful review of electrostatic copying is found in "Preservation Photocopying in Libraries and Archives," *Restaurator* 8 (1987).

a series or collection it may be better to film the entire group, rather than make electrostatic copies, since the microfilm can be used both for preservation and for reference by others.

Microfilming is also preferable to electrostatic copying for orders encompassing all or a substantial portion of a collection or series and for orders containing large numbers of oversized documents, such as maps or blueprints, or large numbers of photographs. Fragile or bound materials that would be damaged by electrostatic copying are excellent candidates for microfilming. Heavily used volumes, collections, and series are often better microfilmed than subjected to repeated use and electrostatic copying.

Microfilming is less damaging than electrostatic copying because materials are supported flat under an overhead camera. It produces a better image in a stable medium, and, most importantly, the negative film may be used to make unlimited numbers of additional copies. Light from repeated electrostatic copying also may damage archival materials. Although some volumes may have to be unbound in order to microfilm them, in many cases, having a permanent preservation copy is an acceptable trade-off. The disbound volume can then be placed in a suitable box and withdrawn from regular use.

Photostatic reproduction and related processes photograph onto paper rather than film. They are most useful for making black and white high contrast images of such large documents as maps, charts, architectural drawings, and newspapers. Older forms created a negative copy from which a positive use copy was made, though newer forms do not involve an intermediate negative. Some photostatic equipment uses an overhead camera so that documents can be supported from underneath, which allows copying of bound newspapers and folded items bound into volumes. Other photostatic equipment uses horizontal cameras that photograph items supported on a copyboard. Photostatic copies are costly because large expensive equipment and skilled technical staff are required.

Electrostatic copying has often superceded photostatic copying. Since it is becoming increasingly difficult to find laboratories that can provide photostatic copying, it is sometimes difficult to make good copies of large items, especially from bound volumes. These processes are still used to copy camera-ready art, so a good source for assistance may be a printer or company that prepares material for printing. Large-screen electrostatic copies can sometimes substitute for copying unbound materials, but machines that roll materials through should be avoided.

Photographic copies are made of historical photographs and of textual and printed materials as well. Users most often request 4″ x 5″ copy negatives and black and white prints in standard sizes: 4″ x 5″, 5″ x 7″, 8″ x 10″, 11″ x 14″, and 16″ x 20″. Some occasionally request larger sizes. Users also request 35 mm slides and color transparencies.

Copyright

In most cases, the making of copies is governed by federal copyright law.[6] Because reference archivists must explain copyright law to users and ensure that copyright is protected, they must understand the concepts applicable to archival copying.

1. Ownership of Copyright. Underlying copyright law is the notion that the creator of a work that embodies unique expression has the right to benefit from the work and to control the public use of this expression. The current copyright law, which was passed by Congress in 1976 and took effect in 1978, applies to any original work of authorship, fixed in tangible form, regardless of format. It includes, therefore, all documentary materials likely to be found in archival and manuscript repositories: manuscripts, photographs, drawings, audiovisual works, sound recordings, and electronic text. The law protects the unique expression of ideas—that is, the exact words or images of the creator—but does not protect the ideas expressed. Documents created by federal government agencies are not protected by copyright and can be copied and published by anyone; state and local governments may copyright materials they create.

Ownership of the copyright in a work is distinct from ownership of the item itself and depends upon the circumstances under which the item was created. Copyright generally belongs to the creator of the work or to his or her heirs. If a work is made for hire, copyright generally belongs to the employer; copyright in the work of a free-lance artist, however, generally belongs to the artist, not to the purchaser of the work.[7] The copyright holder owns a "bundle of rights" that includes the right

- to reproduce the work,
- to make derivative works from it,
- to distribute copies of it,
- to perform it publicly, and
- to display it publicly.

[6] "Copyright," Title 17, U. S. Code. Sections 102, 106, 107, and 108 are reproduced in Appendix 3. For a fuller discussion of the concepts of copyright law, see *Archives & Manuscripts: Law*, especially Chapter 6.

[7] Suzanne Steel, "Copyright News," *SAA Newsletter* (May 1989): 15.

Note that the law grants the right to make copies to the copyright owner and does not distinguish between making one copy and many. Publication is defined as distributing copies.

All works of authorship, whether published or unpublished, are protected by copyright from the moment of creation, whether or not they are marked with copyright notice. To determine the length of time a document is protected by copyright, one must first know when it was created and whether it is published or unpublished. All works created after 1 January 1978, are protected for the life of the author plus fifty years. If the author is not known to have died, but may be presumed to have died, copyright lasts for one hundred years from the date of creation. Copyrights in works published before 1978 and subsisting in January 1978 were extended by a complicated formula outlined in the law.[8]

Unpublished works created before 1 January 1978 that were not copyrighted—which includes the bulk of materials now in archival and manuscript repositories—are protected for the life of the author plus fifty years. For example, a World War II letter written in 1944 by an author who died in 1984 will be protected until 2034. Further, no matter how long ago an author died, all unpublished works created before 1978 are protected for at least twenty-five years after the law took effect, or at least until 31 December 2002. For example, a Civil War letter written in 1864 by a soldier who died later that year will be protected until 31 December 2002. Thus on 1 January 2003, twenty-five years after the current copyright law took effect, a large number of unpublished materials will come into the public domain.

Copyright protection exists whether or not copyright is registered with the Library of Congress, and copyright can be registered at any time. For infringement of copyright in an unregistered work, the copyright holder can recover only actual damages. That is, only direct losses can be recovered. For a registered work, punitive damages can be assessed as well.

Since ownership of copyright is not synonymous with ownership of an item, a repository owns many manuscripts, photographs, and other docu-

Some researchers take notes by hand while others request copies. (*New York State Archives and Records Administration*)

ments for which it does not own copyright. Ownership of copyright must be expressly transferred in writing. Although a donor may retain copyright when giving material to a repository, most repositories ask donors to give their copyrights to the repository. Donors may give copyright in materials they have created, such as their outgoing letters, diaries, drafts of writings, or photographs they have taken. Such a transfer must be expressly made in the deed of gift.

If donors do not own copyright, they cannot give it. The most common example is incoming correspondence. A repository may well own, through a deed of gift from a donor, letters written to the donor by a noted author. Copyright in the letters belongs to the author or the author's heirs, regardless of the ownership of the letters. Ownership of photographic negatives does not necessarily mean ownership of copyright, as many people mistakenly believe. As with other works, copyright in photographs belongs to the photographer—or to the employer if the work was done for hire.[9]

2. Limitations on Rights of Copyright Holders: Fair Use and Copying by Libraries and Archives. Although copyright holders own the bundle of rights, there are limitations on their exclusive rights. One of the most notable, found in Section 107 of the copyright law, is "fair use" of the work for criticism, comment, teaching, or scholarship. It is under this section that archivists and librarians make works available for study. Making copies or publishing quotations without permission from the copyright holder under the fair use provision depends on the context of the use. Four guidelines de-

---

[8] Trudy Peterson says, "The provisos on duration of copyrights subsisting at the time the current law went into effect are wondrously complex. They depend upon whether the copyright was in the first term or in the renewal terms, whether the work was posthumous, whether the work was a composite, and so on." Letter to author.

[9] Steel, "Copyright News," *SAA Newsletter* (May 1989): 15.

fine fair use: the purpose and character of the use, the nature of the material used, the amount of material used in relation to the whole, and the effect of the use on the market for the work. All four tests must be met to allow copying or quotation without permission of the copyright holder.

In Section 108 of the copyright law, another limitation on the rights of copyright holders provides exemption from liability for copyright violation to archives and libraries when they make copies of copyrighted materials, under certain circumstances. They are allowed to make copies of copyrighted works without seeking permission of the copyright holder for two broad purposes—for preservation of holdings and for private use of their patrons. All of the following three conditions must be met to allow copying under Section 108:

- the holdings of the library or archives are open to the public,
- the copies are not made for commercial purpose, and
- notice is given on the copies that the work may be protected by copyright.

A copy of a small portion of a work can be made for a user if the copy becomes the property of the user and notice of copyright is given. A copy of an entire work may be made if the work is not available at a fair price. Section 108b allows archivists to copy an entire document for preservation or for deposit in another research facility.

Both sections 107 and 108 require archivists, curators, and librarians to inform users about copyright law. They must post notice at the place where orders are taken and on order forms. The required notice is found in Figure 7-1.[10] Most repositories require users to sign a statement agreeing to the proper use of copies, and place a copyright statement on copies. It is simplest to place a screen on a copying machine in such a way that all photocopies bear the required copyright notice and the name of the repository, or to use photocopy paper with a notice printed on it. A more time-consuming alternative is to stamp a notice on each copy.

It is important to note that copying without permission of the copyright holder under Section 108 applies only to copying for private research purposes. If archivists have any reason to suspect that the purpose of use is publication or other commercial or public dissemination, they should not make copies

[10] The required notice is found in 37 C. F. R. 201. 14. Also in "Copyright Regulations Require Posted Notices, Warnings on Reproduction Order Forms," *SAA Newsletter* (January 1978): 3.

Figure 7-1   Required Copyright Notice

> NOTICE
> WARNING CONCERNING COPYRIGHT RESTRICTIONS
>
> The copyright law of the United States (Title 17, United States Code) governs the making of photocopies or other reproductions of coyrighted materials.
>
> Under certain conditions specified in the law, libraries and archives are authorized to furnish a photocopy or other reproduction. One of these specified conditions is that the photocopy or reproduction is not be be "used for any purposes other than private study, scholarship, or research." If a user makes a request for, or later uses, a photocopy or reproduction for purposes in excess of "fair use," that user may be liable for copyright infringement.
>
> This institution reserves the right to refuse to accept a copying order if, in its judgment, fulfillment of the order would involve violation of copyright law.

without permission from the copyright holder. Section 108h clearly excludes copying musical works (including sheet music), pictorial works, graphic works, sculpture, films, or audiovisual works without permission for any purpose under this section. Thus, copying photographs without permission under section 108 is certainly restricted.

The two issues of most interest to archivists are the extent to which permission must be obtained from the copyright holder to quote for publication from unpublished materials and the extent to which archivists must have permission from copyright holders to make copies to facilitate research by users. The critical question for archivists arises when users ask to copy some or all of an unpublished work to aid their study. If the repository does not own the copyright, as is usually the case, do archivists require the user to obtain permission before the repository allows copying? For many works it would be difficult if not impossible to locate the copyright holder; is it necessary then to require the user to make a good faith effort to locate the copyright holder before copies are made?

In general archivists have read Section 108 literally, and copied freely for users, as long as the repository meets the three conditions noted above. Archivists used the provisions of Section 108 to argue that copies of entire unpublished manuscripts can be made to aid study without seeking permission of the copyright holder, since no copies are available through normal trade channels at a fair price.[11]

In light of several recent court decisions and the opinions of the Copyright Office, however, it is difficult to advise archivists and manuscript curators with any degree of confidence about applying the provisions of either fair use under Section 107 or copying under Section 108 to unpublished materials commonly found in manuscript collections. Since the early 1980s, the legal concept of fair use and its application to unpublished archival materials has significantly narrowed from common archival and scholarly practice.[12]

Before the 1976 law was enacted, fair use did not apply to unpublished materials; most archivists believed that, under the current law, fair use would apply equally to all copyrighted materials, whether published or unpublished.[13] Recent court cases, however, indicate that the U.S. Supreme Court applies "fair use" differently to unpublished materials. In the case of *Harper and Row v. The Nation,* for example, the Court restricted the application of the doctrine of "fair use" when publishing quotations from unpublished materials, stating that, "The unpublished nature of a work is a key, though not necessarily determinative, factor tending to negate a defense of fair use. And under ordinary circumstances, the author's right to control the first public appearance of his undisseminated expression will outweigh a claim of fair use."[14] In other words, the Court decided that, in the case of unpublished materials, the old common law idea of the right of first publication takes precedence over fair use as defined in the 1976 law.

The U. S. Supreme Court again applied a narrow view of fair use for unpublished materials in the case of *J. D. Salinger v. Random House* (1987) when

it upheld a lower court ruling that author Ian Hamilton could not publish a critical biography of Salinger that included direct quotations from unpublished letters found in manuscript repositories. The Supreme Court agreed that Salinger "has a right to protect the expressive content of his unpublished writings for the term of his copyright. . . ."[15] It is important to note, however, that this decision did uphold the right of repositories to acquire such manuscripts and to make them available for research without the permission of the copyright holder.

Both of these cases dealt with the publication of unpublished materials by users, and limiting publication under fair use only indirectly affects archivists and curators. It is clear that users must seek permission from copyright holders to publish direct quotations from materials in archival custody. Archivists must explain these issues to users and caution them to seek permission to publish. To the extent, however, that archivists relied on fair use to make photocopies for research, the words of the Court distinguishing between published and unpublished materials were somewhat chilling.

Whether an unpublished manuscript item may be photocopied for users to aid research directly affects archivists who must devise policies governing the copying of unpublished materials for use by researchers. Archivists have argued that Section 108 clearly includes copying in archives, and that copyright law no longer distinguishes between published and unpublished works. In marked contrast, the Copyright Office argues that Section 108 applies to unpublished works only when specifically mentioned, as in Section 108b, and that any other copying of unpublished works infringes the author's right of first publication, including the right to control reproduction and distribution. Since some formats such as audiovisual works are specifically excluded from Section 108, one might infer that by implication copying of other materials not excluded, such as textual records, is allowed; but such an argument has not been tested.[16]

---

[11] See for example, Linda M. Matthews, "Copyright and the Duplication of Personal Papers in Archival Repositories," *Library Trends* (Fall 1983): 223-40. Peterson and Peterson, *Archives and Manuscripts: Law,* Chapter 6; Alex Ladenson, "Legal Clinic: Questions and Answers on Copyright," *SAA Newsletter* (May 1979): 8-9.

[12] Useful reviews of these judicial decisions are found in M. Les Benedict, "Copyright I Fair Use of Unpublished Sources/ Copyright II Research and Educational Photocopying," *Perspectives* 28 (April 1990): 1, 9-16; and Ruth Sievers, "Congress Considers Amending Copyright Act's Fair Use Doctrine," *Library of Congress Information Bulletin* 49 (10 September 1990): 309-11.

[13] Michael Crawford, "Copyright, Unpublished Manuscript Records, and the Archivist," *American Archivist* 46 (Spring 1983): 141; Carolyn A. Wallace "Archivists and the New Copyright Law," *Georgia Archive* 6 (1978): 1-17.

[14] *Harper & Row v. the Nation* (471 U. S. 1985 at 555) quoted in Suzanne Flandreau Steel, "Current Copyright Law and the Archivist," *Provenance* 7 (Spring 1989): 1-15.

[15] 7 *Salinger vs. Random House, Inc.,* 811 *Federal Reporter* 2d Series 90 (1987): 100, 95. See also Christopher Runkel, "Salinger v. Random House: The Case," *Constitutional Issues and Archives* (Mid-Atlantic Regional Archives Conference, 1988), 49 60, and Michael Les Benedict, "*Salinger v. Random House:* Implications for Scholars' Use," *Constitutional Issues and Archives* (Mid-Atlantic Regional Archives Conference, 1988), 61-70.

[16] "Statement by Copyright Task Force, Society of American Archivists," in U. S. Copyright Office, *Library Reproduction of Copyrighted Works (17 U. S. Code 108): Report of the Register of Copyrights to the Congress* (Washington, D.C.: Library of Congress, 1983), Appendix iv, Part 2: 89-96. The opinion of the Registrar of Copyright is found throughout *Library Reproduction of Copyrighted Works,* particularly 105-06, 121-24, 329-31.

The court cases cited above, however, appear to side with the conservative opinion of the Copyright Office. The Court seems inclined to protect the rights of the creator of unpublished materials over the rights of users in Section 107. If this reasoning is extended, then making copies under Section 108 may become more difficult. Since the law has been in effect, however, no suit has been brought to test this issue or to prevent archivists and curators from copying unpublished materials without permission from copyright holders, within the limits of the law, under either Section 107 or Section 108.

Archivists must monitor current copyright developments, for they may find themselves in court to test provisions of currently accepted archival reference practice. In the meantime, most repositories, while taking the opinion of the Copyright Office under consideration, continue to make copies for research use, without requiring permission from copyright holders. To protect their repositories, their holdings, and themselves, archivists institute procedures to inform users of copyright law and require users to acknowledge their responsibilities. Some archivists are exploring other options to aid users, such as the expanded use of interlibrary loan and sharing of collections through photocopying.[17]

Repository Copying Policies and Procedures

Although archivists and curators limit photocopying under certain conditions, the archival profession is committed to encouraging the use of archival materials to the greatest extent possible. The guidelines for copying adopted by the Society of American Archivists state unequivocally, "It is the responsibility of a library, archives, or manuscript repository to assist researchers by making or having made reproductions of any material in its possession for research purposes. . . ."[18] Archivists and curators often have mixed feelings about copying: they recognize the importance of copying for the use and dissemination of archival information, but see dangers in unlimited copying, some real and some imagined.

Although recognizing that copying may need to be limited under certain circumstances, the SAA

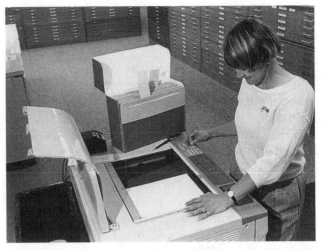

An archives staff member photocopies flagged documents for a researcher. (*Chuck Scheer, courtesy of Special Collections Department, Boise State University Library*)

guidelines do not adequately address the question of limits on the number of photocopies. Copying may be limited, as explained above, for valid legal restrictions on reproduction, such as copyright. Many repositories go beyond copyright restrictions to limit further the number of photocopies that they will make for one user or from one collection. Archivists must determine why the volume of copies is a problem. Is the issue preservation of the originals? Is copying too great a burden on the staff? Or is it that archivists lose control over information? Let us examine each of these questions in turn.

First, copying may harm documents, and the SAA policy states that copying may be limited if the physical condition of the originals would be unacceptably harmed by it. Tightly bound volumes, brittle paper, and oversize scrapbooks may be irreparably damaged by copying. A repository also may specify the type of reproduction that can be made, requiring, for example, microfilm rather than electrostatic photocopies for large numbers of copies, for substantial portions of a collection, if the physical condition is poor, or if awkward size precludes use of a photocopy machine.

In many repositories, staff, not users, make copies. Staff can judge whether physical condition permits copying and ascertain copyright status. Staff copying also reduces the possibility of careless handling, misfiling, or loss. Rather than removing items from collections, users flag documents to be copied to ensure their location and fill out an order form identifying the documents to be copied. Thus, if preservation is the concern, policies and procedures de-

---

[17] Steel, "Current Copyright Law," takes a conservative position. In contrast, Kenneth D. Crews argues that archivists must assert the full rights of fair use to assist scholarship and study, in his "Unpublished Manuscripts and the Right of Fair Use: Copyright Law and the Strategic Management of Information Resources," *Rare Books & Manuscripts Librarianship* 5 (1990): 61-70.

[18] "Statement on the Reproduction of Manuscripts and Archives for Reference Use," *American Archivist* 39 (July 1976): 411. Reproduced in Appendix 2.

veloped to protect documents from unacceptable damage are the solution.

Second, handling copying requests, preparing materials for copying, and the copying itself consume staff time. It is true that some users request many more copies than they will use; they may read only enough to identify material of potential interest and may request copies of entire folders on the basis of folder titles. If staff costs are not recovered in the price set for copying, or if money from copying services is not returned to reference, unlimited copying can distort reference priorities. One way to discourage indiscriminate copying is to set a low fee for small numbers of copies and considerably higher fees for large orders. Thus, if the burden of copying on the staff is the concern, full recovery of costs from users is a better solution than artificial limits on the number of copies.

Third, some archivists and curators object to losing control over access to materials in their custody and believe that unlimited copying means that the contents of archival holdings are scattered, sometimes out of context. Copies of expensive manuscripts have later been given to other repositories, which in turn made the materials available to users for the cost of reproduction. Thus, some archivists fear, perhaps justifiably, that making copies readily available will reduce the number of researchers coming to their repository, thereby lowering the use statistics that justify funding. For these reasons, some archivists limit the number of copies or refuse to photocopy at all, especially if rare or expensive manuscripts are involved.

It is important to note that repositories lose control over the use of *any* information made available to users, whether it is taken from the repository in copies, notes, or the researcher's head. The issue of control is more an issue of access to information than it is one of the volume of copying. If control of information is the issue, then access conditions must be addressed. If information should not be disseminated, it should not be open for research.

In large measure archivists can control this problem: repositories should not accession copies from other institutions without permission from the owner of the original. Likewise they should require users to acknowledge that copies will not be given to another individual or repository without permission, and require all copies to bear the name of the repository. Requests for copies and citations to materials

Microforms are used for research and for preservation. A records manager examines historical drawings on a microfiche reader-printer. (*Thomas F. Lee, courtesy of the Metropolitan Transit Authority, New York*)

can be used to supplement the number of researcher registrations as measures of repository effectiveness.

Thus, limits on copying may be needed for copyright protection or for preservation, and full costs of copying should be recovered; but archivists should not seek to control the flow of information by arbitrary limits on the number of photocopies.

Copying for Mail and Phone Requests. Many users assume that the ready availability of copying means they can write or phone to order copies. The SAA guidelines acknowledge that such requests can overwhelm repository resources. As noted in Chapter 4, a repository is justified in refusing to supply copies if the request requires research by the staff or subjective judgments about the value of material for the user. Each repository should develop guidelines about the amount of time that can be devoted to finding items for users. Since such off-site users also must acknowledge required copyright notices before copies are supplied, the necessary form must be sent to the user, signed, and returned before copies are sent. If charges are to be assessed for searching or copying, users also should be informed of estimated costs and billing procedures before work is performed.

Setting Fees for Copying. Although few repositories charge for use of holdings, nearly all charge for copies. As recommended in the SAA guidelines, most repositories keep fees low to facilitate research. Many also believe that the ready availability of copies discourages theft. Some repositories, however, set high fees for photocopying to discourage indiscriminate copying. Although justified in recovering its copying costs, the repository must decide how much of its costs to recover. The actual costs of copying equipment may be readily calculated, but such indirect costs as staff time and overhead are more difficult to estimate. Many repositories set a minimum charge per order to cover indirect costs. The repository also must specify procedures for payment or billing, delivery or mailing. Staff may need to set priorities among copying orders, especially for large orders or in busy seasons.[19]

Instructions and Order Forms for Copying. Handouts explaining copying policies and copyright law save staff time and help users. Information is needed about

- the types and costs of reproduction available,
- procedures for requesting copies,
- procedures for identifying and flagging documents to be copied,
- billing,
- delivery or mailing,
- the amount of time needed to process orders, and
- an explanation about the costs and procedures of rush orders, if they can be accommodated.

It is best to be very clear about the time required to process orders and to indicate if delays are likely.

Order forms for copying may be simple or complex. In small repositories with limited copying options, one form may suffice. If, however, the repository contracts with several outside laboratories for different types of copying, a separate order form for each may be required. Although handouts may explain to users which forms are appropriate, it is likely that staff assistance will be required to identify the best type of reproduction and to supply all information requested on the form.

Typical order forms include the following elements:

1. Identification of documents to be copied. Space is provided for collection or series title, file unit, title or description of each item, its location in the file, and its page count.

2. Type of reproduction to be made. List the types available to aid researchers in their selection.

3. Copyright notice. The required statement must be printed on all order forms to conform to the law and to ensure all researchers are warned of their obligations.

4. Agreement for use of copies. Users acknowledge that copyright is not transmitted with copies, that they will abide by the law, that they will not transfer the copies to another individual or institution without permission of the repository, and that they will cite the repository as the location of the originals in any exhibit or publication using the materials.

5. Information about price, payment, and delivery. Indicate the total number and cost of copies, method of payment, and method of delivery.

6. Name, address, phone number, and signature of the requester.

7. Date of request, date of completion, name of staff receiving the order.

Order forms are also useful after copying is completed. One copy of the form is sent to the user with the copies; this helps the user identify the copies and cite them correctly. The original signed order form is retained by the repository. If a user misuses copies, signed forms may be important evidence that the repository informed the user of copyright and other use provisions. Since photocopy order forms are an item-level list of selected documents in collections, they can be used to prove ownership in later cases of theft. Order forms also can be used to study how users actually evaluate and select documents during the research process. Order forms are usually filed by name of user. Storing order forms takes space, but they should be kept for as long as the copies are likely to be in active use, at least five years.

Copying Procedures. Most repositories require that copying be done by their staff or by approved laboratories. For electrostatic copying, most

---

[19] A survey of midwestern repositories in 1987 showed a range of photocopying fees from 5 cents a page for self-service copying of selected items in the reading room to 40 cents a page for oversized items copied by the staff. The prevailing rate for copies identified by users and copied by staff, was 10 to 15 cents a page. "Photocopying for Researchers," *MAC Newsletter* (April 1987): 25.

repositories organize their own copying services because of the volume of copying, the relatively low cost of equipment, and the convenience of its ready availability. Some repositories with extensive microfilming or photographic copy work maintain their own laboratories, but most contract with reputable service bureaus or professional photographers to supply copies. Few repositories maintain copy facilities for reproducing motion picture films, videotapes or sound recordings, relying instead upon outside laboratories to perform such work. Users should be informed that they are contracting with an outside laboratory to perform copying, and that the repository cannot guarantee the work of the lab. In some cases a user has established relationships with another laboratory, and the archivist may wish to add it to the approved list after inspection.

In all circumstances, archivists must ensure the safety and preservation of original photographs, negatives, or audiovisual materials. Archivists should visit laboratories from time to time to verify that originals are properly treated while in custody of the laboratory. Photographers, whether in the laboratory or in the repository, must demonstrate by their sensitive treatment of historical documents that they value historical originals. The staff must also ensure that negatives to be retained by the repository are technically sound. Meeting ANSI standards helps ensure photographic quality and preservation standards. Materials must be secure in transit as well as in the laboratory; staff or bonded couriers hired by the repository, not users, should transport materials to off-site processors. Materials must be carefully packaged and protected from rain, rough handling, or extremes of temperature and humidity.[20]

Preparing an order for electrostatic copying is largely done by the user, with assistance from staff if needed. If users flag documents properly and list items clearly on the order form, staff can copy items, folder by folder, efficiently and accurately. Original records are placed by hand on the surface of the copy machine, not fed through an automatic feeder. Photocopying bound documents often damages the spine, especially when pages are forced against a flat platen to get a clear copy of text near the gutter. Some repositories allow users to photocopy unbound materials themselves; if so, it is still wise to require the user to fill out the order form listing the items

copied and to obtain the necessary agreements for use of the copies. As noted above, copyright notice must appear on all copies of materials protected by copyright.

Preparing an order for microfilming is usually more time-consuming. Staff must prepare a table of contents for the entire project if it exceeds one roll and a table of contents for each roll. Filming the inventory for the collection is a good way to provide necessary information. Eye-legible targets are needed at the beginning of each roll of film and of each logical section of material. Items to be microfilmed must be in correct order. Folded documents must be opened and flattened. Missing pages or damaged documents must be noted. Bindings may need to be loosened. Consultation with the camera operator and with a conservator is sometimes needed to ensure a good copy and to reduce stress to the documents. After the filming is completed the film should be checked, frame by frame, against the original materials.[21]

Repositories should always retain the negatives of microfilm and photographs so that additional copies can be made from the negative, and the original need not be subjected to the stress of repeated copying. The copy negative is linked to the original item by a notation made on the original and the finding aid indicating that a negative is available. The negative must be identified and filed in a logical sequence, preferably numerical. Printed lists of existing photographic negatives available for popular subjects and of microfilm publications are a useful reference and outreach tool.

In some circumstances, users are allowed to bring equipment to the repository to make copies themselves. Often photographers and documentary film or video producers ask to bring their own equipment to copy still photographs. To accommodate these requests, copy tables are needed that adequately support items to be copied and only available light should be used. As always, users must sign copyright statements and give negatives to the repository after the project is completed. If these conditions cannot be met, these users should request and pay for photographic copies like other users.

In many repositories, the first researcher to order a copy is charged for both the negative and positive copy even though the archives retains the negative. Creating the negative is the most expensive part of reproduction; subsequent duplicate negatives or positive copies are relatively inexpensive. When

---

[20] In addition to Sung, see Rizenthaler et al.,"Managing a Photographic Copying Service," *Archives and Manuscripts: Administration of Photographic Collections* (Chicago: Society of American Archivists, 1984), 141-52.

[21] Gwinn, *Preservation Microfilming,* 61-95.

reproduction does not create a negative, such as in audio or video taping, a repository may require that two copies be made, one for the user and one for the repository so that the duplicate becomes a use copy. The cost of both is charged to the user.

Users may justifiably protest paying for copies that they do not plan to use, especially when, as in the case of microfilm, the repository requires that an entire volume or series be filmed when a user has requested a substantial part of it. There is no easy solution to this problem; repositories seldom have the resources to film extensively either for preservation or for use. Larger repositories may set up a revolving fund, charging a prorated fee to the first user and charging part of the cost of the master negative to users who later request a copy of the film.

Because of the number and complexity of copying requests, administering copying services can come to dominate reference service. In most cases, copying can be handled by paraprofessional staff. Adequate policies and procedures ensure that copy services meet users' needs and can be accommodated by staff.

Providing Original Documents on Loan

Loans are the exception, not the rule. Often there are acceptable substitutes for loans of original materials. For example, appropriate alternatives to a teacher's request to use original materials in a classroom are a class visit to the repository or multiple facsimile copies of materials for students to use in class and then keep. Other requests for loans can be met with copies, especially administrative requests.

Since a repository will receive loan requests for which no substitute will suffice and since there are circumstances under which loans are acceptable, it must include loan policies in its access policy. A loan is a privilege, not a right; all requests for loans must meet the same standards and follow the same procedures. The archivist should review all loan applications. No matter how eloquent the user's plea or imminent the deadline, there should be no shortcuts in loan procedures. The three most common requests are for administrative use, research use, and exhibition. Some users also may ask to borrow records to make copies with their own copying equipment.

Loans for Administrative Use. Originating agencies may request the temporary return of records for administrative use, and donors may ask to borrow their materials for personal use. Encourage such users to use records at the repository instead of having them returned, or provide copies, especially if the material is to be used for an extended period of time. The instruments documenting the transfer of the records to the archives (deed of gift, deposit agreement, or transfer agreement) should state in some detail the conditions under which records may be recalled, the people in the creating organization or agency authorized to request them, and how far in advance requests should be submitted.

Loans for Exhibition. Exhibitions are important means of conveying information from archives to people unlikely to use them in person. Exhibitions also stimulate public appreciation of history and of the repository and encourage research use. Although copies often can be used for exhibition, the authenticity of original records is an important element in capturing public attention and interest. Museums, libraries, historical societies, or other cultural institutions request loans for exhibition; schools, businesses, or creating agencies may wish to borrow original records for public relations or educational functions. Because of the importance of exhibitions and of the risks they entail, loans for exhibition require considerable scrutiny and careful preparation.[22]

Mary Lynn Ritzenthaler points out that archivists often, in effect, mount informal exhibits when they use attractive or valuable documents for show-and-tell orientation sessions for users, donors, or other visitors. Such use, if repeated frequently, may damage the documents most central to the repository mission. Repositories may protect such documents by keeping a record of their use and condition, encapsulating them, wearing gloves when handling them, or creating facsimile copies for demonstration.[23]

Loans for Research. Repositories should not loan archival materials to individual users, but the expanded use of interlibrary loan might considerably assist individual users and facilitate research. At this time few repositories loan original materials through interlibrary loan, but more might consider it. At a minimum, copies of finding aids can be circulated to other libraries for researchers to use when planning a visit to the repository. Use copies of microfilmed collections or series are also candidates for

[22] Gail Farr Casterline, *Archives and Manuscripts: Exhibits* (Chicago: Society of American Archivists, 1980) discusses all aspects of exhibits including loaning for exhibits.

[23] Ritzenthaler, *Archives and Manuscripts: Conservation,* 62.

The ratification of a state constitution is displayed at a state archives using reproductions of the actual documents. (*Department of Cultural Resources Archives, and Records Section, North Carolina*)

interlibrary loan. Some states, such as Wisconsin, have built networks in which original records are regularly transported to its members, but these networks remain rare.[24]

Loan Policies and Procedures

Requests for Loans. The repository loan policy should indicate how requests are to be formulated and submitted. Applications for loans should be in writing and submitted in time to ensure proper preparation of materials. Requests for return of records

for administrative use should be received at least two weeks in advance of the date of transmittal, and the application should explain why use of the documents in the archives or copies are not sufficient. When possible, the archivist should work with exhibit designers to select materials and to ensure that appropriate preservation and security measures are incorporated into exhibition design. Six months advance notice is not too long to require for a request for exhibition. Repositories may grant exceptions to the time stipulated for simple requests if less time is needed, but sufficient time is needed to respond to large or complicated requests.

The repository's loan policy should specify the environmental conditions under which loaned items are to be used or exhibited. It is helpful to ask the

---

[24] A special issue of *Rare Books and Manuscripts Librarianship* 3 (Fall 1988), presented several papers on lending. Included are Thomas V. Lange, "Alternatives to ILL"; Thomas Hickerson and Anne R. Kenney, "Expanding Access: Loan of Original Materials and Special Collections"; and "RLG Guidelines for Lending".

borrower to complete a checklist describing its physical environment and security procedures. In addition to demonstrating acceptable levels of security, temperature, humidity, and lighting, the borrower for an exhibition must also guarantee safe and acceptable exhibition techniques. Staff of the lending repository may visit the site where the records will be used or exhibited.

A careful examination of requested materials should precede the decision to lend them. The archivist should make a detailed record of the condition of every item before it is loaned for exhibition, perhaps even a photographic record of particularly valuable items. Consultation with a conservator or with a museum accustomed to handling loan requests for exhibition may be warranted in some cases. Less detailed scrutiny is possible for larger groups of records returned for administrative use or for interlibrary loan, but their general condition should be noted.

Some repositories prepare all materials loaned for exhibition and charge the borrowing institution for preparation costs and supplies. They encapsulate or mat items in physically and chemically stable materials and provide exhibit furniture, such as cradles to hold bound volumes.

The duration of the loan is related to the need of the borrower, the condition of the materials, and the physical circumstances of use. It should be as short as possible. As a general rule, only facsimiles, not original archival materials, should be permanently exhibited. Since damage from light exposure is cumulative, it may be necessary to withdraw heavily used items from exhibition.

The policy statement must also spell out how the materials will be packed, insured, and transported and who will carry out and pay for each of these functions. Many repositories pack and transport materials themselves and charge the expenses to the borrower. In some cases, staff accompany the materials to their temporary location.

Loan Agreements. All conditions are recorded in a loan agreement. An appropriate agent of the borrowing agency signs it, verifying the conditions under which the materials will be used and the date of return. The loan agreement also specifies the names of authorized users, the method of transportation, whether copying is permitted, and exhibition techniques to be used. Loan forms must include agreement to meet the stated standards for use of the materials. Borrowers agree that they will not alter materials in any way and will retain original order. The loan policy and agreement should indicate the preferred citation for labels and acknowledgements.

Careful records must be kept of all loans, and the archivist should monitor their status on a regular basis. The repository should request copies of exhibition catalogs or other publications resulting from the exhibition.

* * *

For many users, access to archival materials means obtaining copies or loans of them. Archival repositories are obligated to meet as many requests for copies as possible. Policies and procedures are necessary to simplify the administrative costs of providing copies and to ensure that copyright law is observed. Copies can supply most needs for off-site use of records, but occasionally loans are necessary to meet continuing needs of creating administrators and to enrich exhibitions.

In previous chapters we have examined user needs for intellectual, legal, and physical access to archives. Intellectual access is provided through finding aids and reference assistance. Legal access is defined in the access policy. Physical access is provided in the research room and through copies and loans. To provide access and meet user needs, repositories must organize, administer, and evaluate reference services. These topics are discussed in the next chapter.

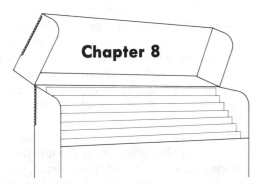

Chapter 8

Managing Reference Services and Evaluating the Use of Archives

To meet users' needs, protect records, and use staff effectively, repositories organize, administer, and evaluate reference services. Staff qualified to provide reference services must be recruited, supervised, and organized in patterns conducive to meeting user needs. Managing reference services requires planning, policies, and procedures. Effective organization and management of reference services also depends on measuring and evaluating the use of archives through routine data collection and user studies. This chapter will discuss organizing and managing reference services and measuring and evaluating the use of archives.

Organizing Reference Services

Repositories typically organize reference staff in one of three models:

    1) a curatorial organization, in which reference services are integrated with arrangement and description, often in a subject or format area;
    2) a rotating organization, in which reference services are provided by all staff members in rotation; and
    3) a functional organization, in which reference services are organized as a separate department.

The effectiveness of each of these arrangements depends on the size of the staff, the size and complexity of the holdings, and the nature of the finding aids. Each model has strengths and weaknesses.

Curatorial Organization. A curatorial organization recognizes that, in provenance-based systems, specialists who arrange and describe records are best qualified to provide reference services for the records since they know how and why the records were created and organized. In a small archives, where one archivist provides all archival services, this ideal may be met. In larger repositories, it is impossible for any one person to be familiar with all holdings, so staff are assigned responsibility for groups of records. Often they are organized on the basis of form, such as audiovisual records, or according to the source of records, such as legislative records.

From the user's point of view, reference services in the curatorial model are dispersed among divisions and may be slighted in the press of other business. Users depend on referrals to appropriate curatorial divisions, and their needs may be fragmented among them. If the subject specialist is absent, reference services may be unavailable. User needs, dispersed and fragmented, may not be identified or considered in overall repository planning. When the curatorial pattern is followed, reference must be integrated with other work of the unit and adequately recognized. Staff development programs to train junior staff and to ensure continuity of reference services and subject expertise are important.

Rotating Reference Services. Many repositories rotate reference activities among staff members on a weekly, daily, or even hourly schedule. All staff have the opportunity to interact with users and to discover how users pose queries and use finding aids and holdings. At the same time, users can benefit from the knowledge of those who acquire, arrange, describe, conserve, and promote the use of records. This model gives administrators maximum flexibility in scheduling work and may provide the staff with welcome diversity in work tasks.

Users, however, may find it difficult to develop rapport or continuing search strategies with a constantly changing staff. If staff fail to give sufficient attention to the substantive intellectual role of the archivist in guiding users, it may well devolve into providing only the administrative aspects of reference services. If all staff rotate, the staff member on duty may have had no experience with the records in use. Staff are less likely to develop expertise or interest in reference activities when the period of service at the reference desk is limited and fragmented. Reference work may come to be seen as an interruption of one's "real" job. If everyone is responsible, it may be that no one is responsible.

Functional Organization. The functional pattern separates reference and public service functions from other functions (appraisal, arrangement and description, and preservation). Reference specialists offer continuity for users from initial interview to follow-up activities. This approach gives reference services an identity and makes reference staff accountable for meeting user needs. Reference specialists can identify the research needs of major user constituencies and develop strategies to meet them. Reference staff can advocate user needs in institutional planning and relay information about user needs to repository staff responsible for acquisitions, processing, or public programs. In some repositories, reference services and public programs are combined in a public services department that systematically anticipates and answers user needs.

In a functional organization reference staff cannot, however, know holdings as well as those who acquire, arrange, and describe them; and, if the acquisitions or processing staff seldom see their work used, they may not understand user needs and perspectives. Because reference staff deal with people all day, every day, they may experience "burnout" and find it difficult to respond imaginatively and patiently to repeated requests. Scheduling can also be a problem, since it may be difficult to staff the reference desk when reference archivists are away. Maintaining communications between technical services and reference staff is critical to making this arrangement work.

In a one-person repository, by necessity, the archivist becomes both subject specialist and reference specialist. In some large institutions, like the National Archives, models are combined: a reference consultant orients users, directs them to appropriate subject specialists, and maintains contact with them throughout research to ensure that all needed divisions are identified and all needed services are provided. In mid-size repositories, the functional division may meet user needs better than staff rotation.

Staff Qualifications. No matter what pattern or combination of patterns is used, service to users must be the foundation of all archival programs. It is critical to staff the reference desk with people capable of meeting the intellectual and personal needs of users. Reference archivists must be knowledgeable about finding aids and holdings. They must understand the history, functions, record forms, and organizations of the records creators, and possess a broad knowledge of the activities documented by repository holdings. Understanding the needs and research methods of major constituencies helps archivists understand their clients. Since appropriate referrals to other information sources are an important element of good service, a sense of the information universe is also necessary, as is familiarity with general reference tools and, increasingly, with on-line bibliographical databases. Reference archivists must be familiar with laws and ethics relating to access and copyright.[1]

Continuing education is important for all professionals, including reference archivists. Time and financial support to attend professional meetings of user groups as well as archival associations, to read new literature in both subject and professional fields, and to undertake user studies and research in repository holdings are imperative.

Although archival administration is a service profession and *all* archivists should have a genuine spirit of public service, a real dedication to public service is especially vital for reference staff, whether professional, para-professional, or clerical. A repository's image is largely shaped by the services provided to users. Reference staff must be able to work with a wide variety of people, treating each request, no matter how mundane or routine, as a fresh question, mustering appropriate interest and assistance. Reference archivists must be particularly aware of the complicated dynamics of interpersonal relationships in archives. Patience, empathy, humor, and good temper are qualities especially important to

---

[1] Janice E. Ruth, "Educating the Reference Archivist," *American Archivist* 51 (Summer 1988): 266-76; and Hugh Taylor, *Archival Services and the Concept of the User* (Paris: UNESCO, 1984).

staff dealing with the public. Public service staff may need education in stress management and in dealing with difficult patrons.[2]

An ability to see process, not products, as the accomplishment of the day also is helpful for reference staff, for there are usually few tangible products to give meaning to each day's work. Instead, the "product" is the less tangible matter of enabling others to pursue their work effectively. Reference staff must be able to adjust to a constantly changing set of priorities in daily responsibilities and be comfortable juggling many demands upon their time. They must be careful and consistent in handling archival materials under the stress of many demands for prompt service.

Many administrative duties can and should be handled by para-professional and clerical staff. Repositories both large and small often employ para-professional reading room attendants to handle such services as registration, retrieval, reshelving, and copying. These support staff may also refer users to appropriate professional staff for intellectual assistance.

Many small repositories, and some large ones, rely on para-professional staff to provide more substantive reference services as well. With some supervision, they can instruct users in the use of finding aids, respond to directional questions, and answer simple factual questions. Likewise, experienced para-professionals may handle some substantive reference questions. Carefully defined search protocols and reference procedures help this arrangement work.

Retaining good employees is important to the quality of reference service. Turnover is particularly damaging because certain kinds of knowledge about holdings can only be gained by experience in the same repository. Establishing clear expectations, helping all employees see how their tasks relate to the larger institutional mission, and acknowledging good work are important keys to staff retention. All positions, professional or para-professional, need written job descriptions outlining responsibilities, authority, and reporting requirements.

Reference services must not become a ghetto where archivists develop subject expertise but are unable to move up a career ladder of increasing administrative responsibility. In many repositories where promotions are based on increased adminis-

trative responsibilities, it is difficult to promote reference staff based on enhanced reference skills gained through study and experience. Repositories can resolve this problem by creating two career ladders, one for increased professional competence and another for greater administrative responsibility.[3]

Managing Reference Services

Managing reference services requires planning, establishing reference policies, implementing policies in procedures, and administering these policies and procedures through records management and time management. It also requires advocacy and communication. These topics will be briefly discussed below.

Planning. Planning for reference services should be integrated into repository planning. Reference staff should identify goals and objectives for reference services and develop an annual workplan that details the activities to be undertaken, the individuals who will perform them, and the needed resources of equipment, money, and space.

Establishing Policies. Establishing policies for reference services rests on repository policies embodied in the access policy. As seen in Chapter 5, policies must be established for access, restrictions to protect privacy and confidentiality, levels of reference services, levels of research services, security, preservation, fees, copying services, loans, and use of information.

Implementing Procedures. A procedures manual that outlines the details of reference procedures saves time and helps ensure that reference practices are consistent. A table of contents listing topics to be covered is shown in Figure 8-1. Maintaining this manual in electronic form makes updating easy.

Records Management. The numerous forms and reference letters generated in providing reference services must be filed and appropriate retention periods determined for them. Most forms are retained in case the archives later discovers theft, abuse, or misuse. Reference records also are used to support requests for reference tools, equipment, staff, and finding aids; and such forms provide the basis for user studies.

Little guidance has been published on the scheduling and disposition of reference records. Re-

[2] Library literature is helpful on this topic. See for example, Rhea Joyce Rubin, "Anger in the Library: Defusing Angry Patrons at the Reference Desk (and Elsewhere)," *Reference Librarian* 31 (1990): 39-51.

[3] Page Putnam Miller, *Developing a Premier National Institution: A Report from the User Community to the National Archives* (Washington: National Coordinating Committee for the Promotion of History, 1989), 23-35.

Figure 8-1   Table of Contents for a Reference Procedures Manual

Overview of Reference Services
  Repository mission statement
  Access policy
  Job descriptions
  Principles of arrangement and description
  Definition of security, preservation, reference, research, public programs
Administration
  Orientation, training, and evaluation of professional staff, support staff, and volunteers
  Scheduling staff for reference service
  Reporting procedures
  Maintaining statistics
  Monitoring and ordering supplies
  List of all forms, their filing and disposition
  List of all brochures, maps, and other handouts
  Instructions on giving directions to repository
  Area map
  Map of repository
  Map of research room, indicating finding aids, equipment
  Hours and services
Finding Aids
  Description of finding aids
  Location of finding aids
  Using finding aids
Registration
  Procedures
  Forms
Interaction with Researchers
  Reference interview
  Continuing assistance
  Exit interview or other follow-up activities
Responding to Inquiries
  Phone inquiries
  Reference letters
  Loan requests
  Requests for permission to publish
  Responding to a subpoena
  Protocols for common questions
Security
  Control of belongings and outerwear
  Limits on amounts of material
  Observing use
Restrictions
  Privacy and confidentiality

Use of facsimiles
List of restricted collections, series, or items
Retrieval and Reshelving Procedures
  Procedures for requesting materials
  Location of all materials
  Control of materials in research room
  Control of materials to be reshelved
  Control of materials to be copied
  Reshelving procedures
  Searching protocols for missing items
  Searching protocols for common searches
Rules for Use of Materials
  Rules for use by researchers
  Rules for use by staff
  Textual materials
  Photographic materials
  Microfilm
  Special forms
Equipment
  Using audiovisual or other special equipment
  Maintaining equipment
Duplication
  Electrostatic photocopying
  Microfilming
  Photographic copying
  Photostatic copying
  Audiovisual duplication
  Price lists and order forms
Emergencies
  Fire
  Suspected theft or abuse of materials
  Power outage
  Natural disasters, such as earthquake, tornado
  Medical emergency—staff or researcher
  Disoriented or disorderly researcher
Orientation Sessions
  Scheduling
  Preparing
  Conducting
Other Public Programs
  Exhibits
  Lectures
  Conferences
Appendices
  Examples of all forms
  Examples of all handouts

searcher registration forms are usually filed by name of user in an annual file and kept for as long as possible. Request forms are filed and kept as long as possible to provide evidence in case of theft or abuse of records. The National Archives keeps both registration forms and call slips for twenty-five

years. Photocopy request forms also are retained because they require a signature by which the user agrees to abide by copyright law. If later publication exceeds fair use, the repository will want to show that it warned the user. One repository keeps all reference letters for five years, filed in annual files,

Figure 8-2 Tracking Requests

```
Directed to staff member (name) _____
Date directed _____
Name of researcher _____
Type of request
      Letter __ Phone Call __ Copying __
Notes _____
      _____
      _____
```

Courtesy Michigan Historical Collections, Bentley Historical Library, University of Michigan

thereunder alphabetically by user. After five years, routine reference letters are destroyed; significant correspondence is kept indefinitely.

Time Management. Time management in reference is difficult, but because of that very difficulty, it is vital. In the research room the time constraints of staff and users intersect and sometimes conflict. The larger the reference staff and the more numerous the users, the more complicated time management becomes. Time must be managed in the context of institutional mission and resources outlined in the access statement. Although regrettable, the reality is that no repository can be all things to all actual or potential users. Each repository must acknowledge its limitations of staff and budget and establish policies that serve the greatest number in terms of its overall mission. At the same time the repository can work to identify unmet needs and seek resources to meet them. Priorities must be set as rationally as possible; it is unfair both to users and to reference archivists to make such decisions on an ad hoc basis.

Scheduling reference staff can be difficult because it is impossible to predict the volume of users and the complexity of their requests on any given day. Good recordkeeping through such tools as the registration form and daily log, however, enables the reference archivist to identify patterns in research volume and substance and to plan staffing allocations to meet them. For a large reference staff, it is helpful to use a tracking system, as shown in Figure 8-2, to monitor responsibility for each reference letter, phone inquiry, or photocopy request. Each slip is filed by name of the staff member to whom the work is assigned.

Reference staff constantly seek ways to make best use of their time and to make reference more efficient and effective. One-to-one reference service may be the best way to meet certain user needs, but different solutions may be more effective to meet

others. For example, if extensive and increasing reference assistance is needed for a particular body of records, allocating staff to create a folder title list or an index may decrease the need for reference assistance. If numerous new users need extensive assistance, increasing the number of staff assigned to the reference desk is not the only solution and may not be the best. Developing educational programs such as Saturday workshops in research methods, creating brochures describing research strategies for common problems, or producing an introductory videotape describing archival procedures may be a more effective use of time.

Automation makes reference work more effective by capturing information largely in the heads of archivists, by freeing users from dependence on mediation by archival staff, and by allowing users to improve archival description. It can also be used to create standard responses to frequent requests, and reduce the amount of time spent on routine administrative tasks like registering users, keeping track of materials in the research room, and filing registration forms and request slips.

Advocacy and Communication. Reference archivists are advocates for the needs of users in repository planning, meeting regularly with upper management to report on use and user needs. Reference archivists also communicate user needs to other staff. Arguing for adequate space and equipment, sufficient number of well-trained staff, usable finding aids, appropriate public programs, and useful publications is an important reference responsibility.

In larger repositories scheduled staff meetings of department heads provide for structured discussion of departmental needs. Reviewing the accessions log regularly keeps reference staff aware of new holdings; in turn, reference requests may suggest leads for possible acquisitions. Reference staff should read finding aids in draft and comment freely on them. In turn, processing staff find that reading reference letters keeps them aware of user needs; they also might answer queries relating to their specialty.

Measuring and Evaluating the Use of Archives

"What is the use of archives?" Bruce Dearstyne has asked. Many ask this question implicitly, if not explicitly. Sometimes the question refers to the activities of searching, reading, and noting information in archives. More frequently, however, the question means, "What is the value of preserving historical records?" To respond to the question in either of its meanings, archivists must measure and evaluate the use of archives at three levels.[4]

At the level of the reference function, measuring the use of repository holdings is necessary to organize and manage reference services in the repository and to evaluate their effectiveness. Information about use and users is needed to allocate resources, plan staffing patterns, order equipment and supplies, plan programs to meet identified needs, and reward staff. Such information helps staff to determine whether the level of service is adequate, assess assumptions about reference services, and modify services to meet changing circumstances. Qualitative assessments of service outputs are needed to evaluate such attributes as promptness, thoroughness, courtesy, care, and adequacy of response. Meaningful evaluation of reference services compares performance with some standard—either repository objectives or professional standards.

At the repository level, understanding the use of the holdings is necessary to plan the work of the repository and to advocate support for it. Information about use of the repository is used to plan descriptive programs, set processing priorities, develop acquisition strategies, and plan public programs. Quantitative and qualitative measures are necessary to justify the value of archives to resource allocators.

At the broadest level, understanding and publicizing the use of archives contributes to greater public understanding of the value of preserving archives and the necessity of supporting archival and manuscript repositories. It also facilitates planning cooperative programs to carry out the archival mission, such as documentation strategies to preserve records of enduring value and national bibliographic systems to enhance accessibility. Examination of the uses of archives by all archivists will contribute to the development of standards of practice for the profession.

Paul Conway suggests that archivists should measure and evaluate three aspects of the use of archives: quality, value, and integrity.[5] Conway's framework for studying the uses of archives, shown

in Figure 8-3, provides a useful structure for discussing evaluation. He defines this framework as follows:

1. Quality: How well do archivists understand and meet the information needs of users? To understand quality, archivists both measure user needs and evaluate the quality of reference services.

2. Value: What are the effects of use on individuals, groups, and society as a whole? To understand value, archivists assess the value of archival information to researchers and to indirect users beyond the repository.

3. Integrity: How well do archivists balance their obligations to preserve materials against their obligations to make them available? The purpose of many of the forms used to manage reference service is security. Information gathered in them can be used, beyond security, to plan preservation and reproduction programs.

Since security and preservation have been considered in previous chapters, the following discussion will focus first on understanding user needs and evaluating the quality of reference service. Understanding the value of archives will be considered later in the chapter.

Evaluating Quality: Understanding User Needs. On the simplest level, understanding user needs begins with measuring the use of the repository. Developing quantitative measures of use is relatively straightforward for they are built into the daily work of the reference department. The many "forms, forms, forms" used in providing reference services generate a wealth of data to measure and evaluate them. Some data are supplied by users, for example, in registration forms. During the course of research visits, users supply information that can be analyzed to see how they structure their research at the repository. Request slips document what records are requested; photocopy forms suggest where users expect to find useful information. Reference staff supply other data, for example, in the phone log or exit interviews.

The Society of American Archivists and the National Association of Government Archivists and Records Administrators recommend keeping daily measures of users and of materials used, copied, or loaned, and aggregating them monthly, quarterly, and annually. These measures are shown in Figure

[4] Bruce Dearstyne, "What is the Use of Archives? A Challenge for the Profession," *American Archivist* 50 (Winter 1987): 76-87.
[5] Paul Conway, "Facts and Frameworks: An Approach to Studying the Users of Archives," *American Archivist* 49 (Fall 1986): 393-407.

Figure 8-3   Framework for Studying the Users of Archives

METHODOLOGY

OBJECTIVES		Stage 1 **Registration** (all users/always)	Stage 2 **Orientation** (all users at selected times)	Stage 3 **Follow Up** (sample users/selected times)
	Quality	Nature of Task • *definition in terms of subject, format, scope*	Preparation of Researcher • *experience* • *stage of defined problem* • *basic/applied* Anticipated Service	Search Strategies and Mechanics • *search order* • *posing search*
	Integrity	Identification • *name* • *address* • *telephone* Agree to Rules	Knowledge of Holdings and Services • *written sources* • *verbal sources*	Intensity and Frequency of Use • *collections used* • *time spent with files*
	Value	Membership in Networks • *group affiliation* Can We Contact You? Can We Tell Others?	Intended Use • *purpose in terms of function and product*	Significant Use Significant Info • *importance of archives* • *other sources* • *valuable information* • *gaps in information*

METHODOLOGY

OBJECTIVES		Stage 4 **Survey** (random sample)	Stage 5 **Experiments** (special groups)
	Quality	Expectations and Satisfaction • *styles of research* • *approaches to searching* • *levels of service*	Access and Non-use • *Frustration indexes* • *perceptions of use*
	Integrity	Alternative to Physical Use • *value and use of microforms* • *value and use of databases*	Format Independence • *linkages with information creation* • *technology and information*
	Value	Impact of Use • *increased use* • *citation patterns* • *decision-making*	Role of Historical Information in Society • total potential demand • community network anaylsis

Paul Conway, ''Facts and Frameworks: An Approach to Studying the Users of Archives,'' *American Archivist* 49 (Fall 1986): 397.

Figure 8-4 Quantitative Measures of the Use of Archives

Counts of users:
   1) number of different persons using the repository;
   2) number of daily visits (sum of the daily counts of users who spend all or part of any day in the repository);
   3) number of requests received by phone; and
   4) number of requests received by mail:
Measurements of materials used:
   5) number of retrievals;
   6) number of collections/record groups/series used; and
   7) amount of material used, measured in feet or in number of volumes or continers.
Measurements of materials copied or loaned:
   8) number of pages photocopied;
   9) number of microform images dupicated;
   10) number of photographs duplicated;
   11) number of sound recordings duplicated (by type and unit);
   12) number of machine-readable storage units duplicated (by type and unit); and
   13) number of loans and number of items loaned.

8-4. Information also should be collected about the number of full time equivalent employees (FTE's) devoted to reference activity including professional, para-professional, and clerical staff.[6]

Simply collecting data is not enough; it must be used. A repository can use statistical information to follow patterns of use within the repository. For example, graphing the number of daily visits over a year helps to understand seasonal patterns of use and assists in assigning staff; charting the total number of users over several years can indicate whether use is growing or declining; and knowing the number and types of copies is necessary to order equipment and supplies.

Understanding user needs and the configuration of use in a particular repository, however, requires analysis of information beyond these statistics. Some demographic information collected from all users—in registration forms, call slips, photocopy forms, user evaluation forms, or exit interviews—should be aggregated and analyzed periodically in monthly, quarterly, and annual reports. It provides a basis for studying user needs and the nature of use.

Regularly analyzed registration variables include the types of users, the institutions they represent, and their geographical distribution. Meaningful and discrete categories of users or queries to be analyzed must be carefully defined, and will vary according to repository mission. Categories can reflect occupational characteristics of users, such as staff from the parent institution, students from the parent university, or faculty from other universities. Institutional archives may wish to categorize organizational departments represented, such legal, corporate communications, or advertising. However structured, such analysis should identify user groups in terms of institutional mission and follow changes over time, so that archivists can measure how well they are meeting user needs.

In addition to the large amount of information collected directly from all users, it is helpful to seek other information periodically from all or from a random sample of users. For example, Conway suggests gaining additional information about sources consulted and research approaches used from samples of users.[7]

Information about use provides important feedback to other archival functions. Analyzing registration information to study how people find out about the repository, how they decide whether to visit, and what types of questions they ask can be used to evaluate effectiveness of descriptive programs. As use of automated databases increases, it is important for archivists to understand "user presentation language," that is, the wording of the user's initial query.[8] This will enable archivists to design databases with search capabilities that better meet user needs. Registration information about search categories, such as legislative history or genealogy, or about formats sought, such as textual records or visual materials, may be used to determine the effectiveness of acquisition programs or to structure public programs.

To reach new constituencies and better serve under-represented ones, the repository must collect information from *potential* users. For example, institutional archivists have much indirect evidence at hand about potential users; they have an unparalleled opportunity to use their own holdings to analyze patterns of information creation, use, and transfer in the parent institution. Such research could be the basis for a focus group discussion with targeted

---

[6] Society of American Archivists Task Force on Standard Reporting Practice, "Final Report," *SAA Newsletter* (November 1983):13-16; Task Force on Institutional Evaluation, *Archives Assessment and Planning Workbook* (Chicago: Society of American Archivists, 1989); National Association of Government Archivists and Records Administrators, *Program Reporting Guidelines for Government Records Programs* [1987].

---

[7] Conway, "Facts and Frameworks," 404.

[8] David Bearman, "User Presentation Language," *Archives and Museum Informatics* 3 (Winter 1989-90): 3-7.

Figure 8-5   Qualities Associated with Good Reference Service

Behavioral Characteristics	**Knowledge of**
• approachability	• the parent organization
• sense of willingness	• the acquisitions policy
• a friendly attitude, neither condescending or didactic	• functions of record creators and forms of recordkeeping in parent organization
• ability to communicate orally and in writing	• holdings
• acknowledgement of users who are waiting	• finding aids
• determination to do a good job	• recordkeeping technologies
• ability to deal effectively with problem personalities	• handwriting, dating conventions, terminology used in documents
• positive response and attitude towards questions	• equipment needed to use record forms
• alertness to users needing help but not asking for it	• preservation and security issues
Reference Skills	• how to use and preserve different record forms
• effectiveness in interviewing: getting to user's real questions, getting full and accurate statement of need	• when and how to refer users to other sources
• thorough investigation of a problem	• reference services offered (searching, copies, loans)
• ability to know when only a short answer is appropriate	• repository resources and time limitations
• providing and explaining search strategy to user	• research methodologies and characteristics of queries of major constituencies of repository
• systematic approach	• laws and ethical principles governing access and use of information
• awareness of not knowing the answer and when to refer	• copyright law
• development of methodology for answering "unanswerable" questions	• repository policies
• clear logical questions	• communications networks with other information sources
• ability to use all resources available, archival, library, audiovisual, computer, and telephone	
• ability to buy time when needed	
• investigative know-how	

Adapted, with permission, from Diane G. Schwartz and Dottie Eakin "Reference Service Standards, Performance Criteria, and Evaluation," *Journal of Academic Librarianship*, 12 (1986): 4-8.

administrators examining their need and use of information and their perceptions of archival holdings and services. Such discussions could identify programs or specialized reference services that would enable administrators to make better use of archival holdings. Similarly, a historical society might develop focus group sessions with genealogists to identify their needs, or survey faculty of local university departments of history, political science, and sociology to determine both their research interests and teaching methods.

Evaluating Reference Services. When evaluating how well archivists meet the information needs of users, there are two aspects to consider: individual performance and repository performance. Both aspects can be evaluated by users through exit interviews, evaluation forms, and follow-up surveys,

and by staff through peer observation and assessment.

Evaluating performance of reference staff members requires assessment of personal behavior, knowledge, and reference skills. A repository can formulate a checklist of desirable qualities, as in Figure 8-5, and rate individual performance periodically, using reference service standards, as outlined in Figure 8-6.[9]

Evaluating repository performance requires assessment of such qualitative factors as accessibility, quality of finding aids, comfort, quality of holdings,

---

[9] Diane G. Schwartz and Dottie Eakin, "Reference Service Standards, Performance Criteria, and Evaluation," *Journal of Academic Librarianship* 12 (1986): 4-8; Jane P. Kleiner, "Ensuring Quality Reference Desk Service: The Introduction of a Peer Process," *RQ* 30 (Spring 1991): 349-61.

Figure 8-6   Standards for Reference Services

> A reference archivist conveys an attitude and manner that encourages users to seek assistance.
>
> Assistance is provided at the appropriate level of need. A reference archivist:
>
> —Determines real question; continues questioning to be sure the problem is understood;
>
> —Makes certain that the user knows how to use the sources identified, provides needed instruction in use of finding aids and sources;
>
> —Suggests alternative sources, including other repositories or departments;
>
> —Suggests services when appropriate and offers pertinent information about them, even if not directly requested;
>
> —Answers questions within time requirements of user.
>
> Reference archivists have a thorough knowledge of holdings and finding aids.
>
> Reference archivists are able to plan and execute effective search strategies for complex or extended research problems.
>
> Repository services and policies are understood and described to users whenever appropriate.

Adapted, with permission, from Diane G. Schwartz and Dottie Eakin, "Reference Service Standards, Performance Criteria, and Evaluation," *Journal of Academic Librarianship*, 12 (1986): 4-8.

accuracy of information provided, costs, timeliness, and other aspects of user satisfaction. After a research visit, users can be asked to evaluate the quality of service. How well did archival reality meet initial expectations? How satisfactory were services, finding aids, and holdings? How well did the reference system perform in relation to user information problems? Such information can be requested directly from users during exit interviews, through user evaluation forms, or through other follow-up activities after the visit. The checklists found in the *Archives Planning and Assessment Workbook*, can also be used to assess repository performance.[10]

Understanding the Value of Use. Developing measures of the value of the use of archival materials of and the information they contain is more problematic than evaluating the quality of reference service. To understand the effects of use on individuals, groups, and society as a whole, one must determine exactly what is to be measured and then how to measure it. It is dangerous to measure the value of archives only by the number of direct users since

archival and manuscript repositories will never be able to justify necessary support by quantitative comparisons to libraries or other public programs. Indeed, archivists must guard against measuring use of archives simply by activities in the reading room since the indirect use of archives occurs in an unknown number of other settings.

Bruce Dearstyne has suggested two standards for evaluating the significance of use.[11] The first is the significance of the use in terms of the repository's mission and priorities. As seen in Chapter 5, every repository should have a mission statement outlining its purpose and the types of research it is founded to support. This statement is the basis for the access policy. In determining repository policies, a publicly funded state archives must decide, for example, whether large numbers of instate genealogical researchers, working for personal ends, are more or less significant than a handful of nonresident scholars publishing research in specialized journals. It is important to reiterate that no one should be denied access to materials because of the nature of their research or their occupational status, although level of services may vary.

Dearstyne's second basis for evaluating the significance of use is the significance of the subject and the dissemination of its results. Here the focus is on the indirect uses of the information. Archivists can assess dissemination and use of archival information by asking users to identify the intended products of their research and by undertaking follow-up studies of the use of information. (See Figure 8-7) Archivists also can study the products of research to determine where information goes and how it is used after it leaves the archives through such tools as citation analysis.[12]

User Studies. User studies are tools that can be used to gain greater understanding of any one of Conway's three variables: quality, value, or integrity. Many repositories have the data and resources to undertake systematic user studies. (See Figure 8-8). User studies can focus on one repository or analyze regional, state, or national patterns. Whether used to measure quality, integrity, or value, user

---

[10] *Archives Planning and Assessment Workbook* (Chicago: Society of American Archivists, 1989). Section 9 "Access Policies and Reference Services" is reproduced in Appendix 4.

[11] Dearstyne, "What is the Use of Archives?" 80.

[12] Examples of such studies include Fredric Miller, "Use, Appraisal, and Research: A Case Study of Social History," *American Archivist* 49 (Fall 1986): 371-92; Jacqueline Goggin, "The Indirect Approach: A Study of Scholarly Users of Black and Women's Organizational Records in the Library of Congress Manuscripts Division," *Midwestern Archivist* 11 (Summer 1986):

Figure 8-7 Follow-up Questionnaire for Users of Archives

1. Did you find the information that you sought?
   ___ yes ___ no
2. How important or significant was the information for your purposes? ___ Very important ___ somewhat useful ___ not at all useful
3. Was the information generally used:
   a. as illustration?
   b. to support one or more major points?
   c. to support several major parts of the project?
   d. as the basis for the entire project?
4. Did the information lead you to a new interpretation for the project? ___ yes ___ no
5. Did the information lead to other sources for your project? ___ yes ___ no
6. Did you submit the results of your research for publication? ___ yes ___ no
7. Was it published? ___ yes ___ no
   Article Title _____
   Publication _____
   Volume, date, page _____
   Book Title _____
   Publisher _____
   Place and date _____
8. Did you take the information to a family reunion?
   ___ yes ___ no
9. Did you distribute it as a memo or report?
   ___ yes ___ no
10. Was it used in a lecture or speech? ___ yes ___ no
11. Did you use it in an exhibit, film, or videotape?
    Title _____
    Publisher _____
    Date _____
12. Was it used by a client? ___ yes ___ no
    If so please explain _____

studies, like other research projects, have common elements.[13]

1. Choose the question to be studied. What does the repository want to know and why? Is it how best to reach a new constituency or how to better meet the needs of a current constituency? What collections are most used? How adequate are initial and exit interviews? How effective are current finding aids? What is the effect of automation on use? What are the implications of automation for training staff and users?

2. Define the population to be studied. Who will be the subjects of the study: potential users, all current users, or subgroups of current users such as students, genealogists, or staff of the parent institution?

3. Decide the research method to be used. The desired use of the study should determine the research method. Some methods provide data that describe current behavior; others provide data that explain causes of behavior. And others enable the researcher to make generalizations about group behavior based on the study of a smaller population.

—In a *census,* the archivist asks the same questions of all the subjects in the population to be studied. Registration forms are like a census in that the same information is collected from all users of a repository.

—In a *survey,* the archivist poses questions to a sample from the larger group. If the sample is chosen randomly, the archivist may generalize findings from the sample to the larger group from which the sample is taken. For example, a follow-up questionnaire about the use of archival sources might be sent to a random sample of registered users.

—In a *panel study,* the archivist follows a group of individuals over time to study how they use sources. This might work well following a group of college or graduate students through their course of study.

—*Case studies* provide in-depth analyses of members of one group.

—*Focus group interviews* typically probe for motivation, seeking to understand research behavior or the psychological dynamics of reference transactions. Focus groups may also provide preliminary information that can be used to define research questions for more rigorous study.

—*Field experiments,* although rare in information settings, may become more viable because the logs of some automated retrieval systems allow for laboratory-like analysis of user behavior in searching databases.

4. Gather and analyze data. Some data can be analyzed by simple paper-and-pencil aggregations and ratios. For example, a measure of intensity of use can be obtained by dividing the total volume of holdings by the total number of daily visits in a year.

[13] Paul Conway presented this framework in an SAA workshop, "Users and Use: Planning a Research Program For Archives," 28 September 1988, Atlanta, Georgia. See also Ronald R. Powell, *Basic Research Methods for Librarians* (Norwood, N. J.: Ablex Publishing, 1985); and Meredith Butler and Bonnie Gratch, "Planning a User Study—The Process Defined," *College and Research Libraries* 43 (July 1982): 320-30.

Figure 8-8   User Studies in Archives

Point of Contact	Method of Contact	
	Direct Contact	**Indirect Contact**
Pre-Visit (Getting to potential users)	Community analysis Focus groups	Citation anaylsis Records management
Actual Contact	Reference logs Registration Initial interview Exit interview Observation	Call slip analysis Photocopy requests Time motion studies of staff
Post-Visit	Telephone follow-up Follow-up survey	Citation analysis

Suggested by Paul Conway.

A simple measure of reference demand can be obtained by dividing the annual total of daily visits by the number of full-time-equivalent employees (FTE's) devoted to reference activity. Using registration forms to compute the total number of visitors from particular institutions or geographical areas may be useful in planning public programs: institutions with few representatives may be targeted for further study to determine why the underrepresentation occurs and to suggest public programs to increase use. Other data may best be handled by using statistical packages that allow for more sophisticated analysis.

5. Report, circulate, and use findings. The archivist assembles the results of studies into reports that are circulated to other members of the repository staff or administration. This data will be the basis for improving reference services or public programs. User studies also should be circulated to members of the archival profession through papers and articles. Much more research is needed to understand how users approach and use archives.

* * *

Repositories must acknowledge the centrality of reference services to the mission of the archival repository and determine the most effective means of organizing staff to provide necessary services to users. Evaluating reference services at both the individual and departmental level is important to maintaining and improving their quality and effectiveness. Measuring and assessing patterns of use in a given repository is important for planning and evaluating reference services and is an important part of repository planning and profession-wide research. User studies also form the basis for planning public programs to promote the wider use of archives.

Chapter 9

The Future of Reference Services in Archives

Although it is difficult to predict the future of reference services in archives, the outlines of changes in intellectual, legal, and physical access to information can be discerned. Automation, a major revolution well under way, is greatly expanding archivists' ability to provide intellectual access, especially information about holdings. The participation of many repositories in national online bibliographic networks such as RLIN and OCLC has already made more information about archives available to a wider research public than could have been envisioned a decade ago. Inventories, registers, and other in-house finding aids are increasingly produced using word processing systems. Some repositories use word processing systems to produce indexes for inventories, and other repositories employ full-text searching of these finding aids.

Automation will make some users much more self-sufficient; it will necessitate more reference assistance for others. Many users, lacking computer skills or access to hardware, will still depend on reference archivists to help them interact with automated systems. Understanding the information needs and research methods of significant users of archives is more important as archivists have the technology to create new finding aids.

Many large university and public libraries describe all formats—including visual materials, archives, and manuscripts—in one integrated, online catalog. These systems sometimes do not provide meaningful information about archives and manuscripts. For example, bibliographic entries created to describe books, such as authors and titles, are not always strictly analogous with archival entries such as record creators and series descriptions. Such entries may be confusing to online users, and since terminals can be located anywhere, there is no one knowledgeable to ask for more information.

Users, such as students and the general public, who have not thought of asking for archival materials, now find citations to archives and manuscripts displayed on terminals along with books and periodicals. Yet most novice users are unprepared for the complexities of using archives; they will still depend on archivists despite automation. Even experienced users may rely on reference archivists to provide road maps through the forest of citations produced by online databases. Determining a search strategy for approaching archival materials and providing the context for understanding them are likely to remain important reference services.

There are many unresolved issues relating to automation. It is not yet clear how the costs of providing automated access will be allocated, nor how users outside bibliographic networks will gain access to them. At the present time, access to both major national bibliographic utilities is necessary to search for information about all reported holdings since some repositories belong to RLIN and others to OCLC.

New technologies for controlling information about holdings may in fact alter the very methods by which archivists arrange and describe records. In some repositories, the record group is no longer used as an intellectual construct for organizing records, and the inventory is no longer the primary finding aid. These tools have been replaced by an online database that describes and links records creators and series. Automation may blur the distinction between reference and processing staffs, since reference archivists can now update automated finding aids to reflect additional information acquired during use.

Automation also raises issues affecting legal access. In an age when information about individuals is collected, stored, and linked through databases, little individual privacy may be left. Information about telephone calls, credit card purchases, airline reservations, medical insurance, and student grades are only a few examples of information stored in electronic form. Insuring the proper use of such personal information will become even more critical as the reach and power of these tools increases.

Another revolution well under way affects the storage and transmission of information from archival holdings, rapidly altering the conditions of physical access. Reference requests may be received and answered via electronic mail or facsimile ("fax") machines. Administrative reference in institutional archives may be expanded if archives are linked to local area networks (LANs) within the parent institution.[1] It is clear that in the future archivists increasingly will be linked to users via telecommunication networks.

Reference archivists can use automation to administer the research room more effectively. Already word processing is used to create "boiler-plate" responses to common reference queries. Registration of users, and retrieval and control of materials in use can also be automated. Much of the routine information now collected on forms can be automated through the use of light pens and bar codes.

Records in electronic form can be copied, and the copies reorganized, reformatted, and transmitted without altering the original record. In some archives it is possible to link computers so that archival data in electronic form can be copied and transmitted for use at another site.

The availability of optical disks, CD-ROM, and other storage media make it possible to store, retrieve, and use archival information in a wide variety of settings off-site. CD ROM offers large, inexpensive, storage space that can be readily copied. Data can be loaded into personal computers, searched, manipulated, and printed. The massive increase in the volume of information in archives in recent decades may be paralleled by increasing speed of dissemination in years to come.

Reference service may be redefined in ways yet unseen. It is probable that reference archivists will be called upon to provide information rather than records. They may design and refer to electronic databases that remain in the physical custody of the creating agency. Charles Dollar states, "Redefined reference service involves the promotion of access through the adoption of software interface tools and information exchange standards. The primary software tool here is likely to be a standardized information resource directory system, which will contain crucial information about an information system and also will facilitate cost-effective migration of complex information systems (metadata and records) across technologies, which helps mitigate the problems of technology obsolescence."[2]

Reference archivists, like all archivists, have begun to realize the vital necessity for advocacy and for educating records creators, records users, and the general public about the value of archives. Reference archivists shape the image of their repository. But more, they can make archives accessible and valued by making the collective memory of an organization readily usable by current staff, by studying the dissemination of information from archives, by analyzing the common characteristics of information seeking behavior of major user groups to improve finding aids, and by reaching out to potential users.

Whatever the future brings, the joint quest of users and archivists to find patterns in the past that have meaning for the present will persist. Reference archivists share with users an enthusiasm for historical research because they feel the necessity of understanding the past to make sense of the present and to plan for the future. Archival research is "shared by archivist and user alike, both bending their skills toward wrestling knowledge from information and wisdom from knowledge in this troubled world."[3] Recorded memory is vital to cultural continuity. "It is a hallmark of human societies that they seek to preserve a memory of the past, and have always done so. Indeed, keeping and using the past is central to our concept of human cultures and civilization."[4]

---

[1] Glen A. Gildemeister, "Automation, Reference, and the Small Repository, 1967-1997," *Midwestern Archivist* 13 (1988): 5-15.

[2] Charles Dollar, "Archival Theory and Practices and Informatics: Some Considerations," paper delivered at The University of Macerata, Italy, 7 September 1990.

[3] Hugh Taylor, *Archival Services and the Concept of the User*, 89.

[4] David Bearman, *Archival Methods* (Pittsburgh: Archives and Museum Informatics, 1989), 1.

Reference archivists contribute to individual growth and understanding, to the solution of practical social problems, to scholarly research, and to cultural continuity. They empower individuals and groups by helping them to link their past and future. Reference work calls for ingenuity and perseverance. It depends on the virtues of patience, attentiveness, understanding, and sympathy. At its best, reference work brings forth the meaningful association of information and insights that result in new understanding of the human condition. Reference archivists breathe a second life into records, and do indeed "make them feed the mind of Man."

Bibliographical Essay

General Works

Reference services were slow to develop an identity in archival administration, and the literature about them is underdeveloped in comparison with other archival functions, although not as thin as an initial search under the term "reference services" might indicate. This comparative lack of attention may result from the common assumption that reference services are placed at the end of a continuum of activities that begin with the creation of the records in the originating office (shaped by records management) followed by appraisal, accessioning, arrangement, and description, concluding with reference services and outreach activities. Driven by the need to manage and protect large quantities of records, archivists primarily thought of reference services as a series of administrative decisions made after records have been appraised, accessioned, arranged, and described.

Much of the literature about reference services focuses on the externalities of the relationship between user and repository, that is, on the administration of reference services such as registration, security, paging, storage, retrieval, and photocopying, or on legal aspects of access such as privacy, restrictions, and copyright. As suggested in earlier chapters, reference services in archives go far beyond these administrative elements. Much of the literature relevant to reference services has been cited in the footnotes; this essay considers works cited earlier, as well as others.

Few monographs are devoted to reference services in archives. The first one, succinct and still useful, is Sue Holbert, *Archives & Manuscripts: Reference and Access* (Chicago: Society of American Archivists, 1977). A broad overview is offered by Hugh Taylor in his *Archival Services and the Concept of The User: A RAMP Study* (Paris: UNESCO, 1984; ERIC Document ED 246 906). An international perspective is offered by Michel Duchein, *Obstacles to the Access, Use and Transfer of Information from Archives* (Paris: UNESCO, 1983).

Other overviews of reference services appear as chapters in more general works. Standard works

include T. R. Schellenberg, "Reference Service," *Modern Archives: Principles and Techniques* (Chicago: University of Chicago Press, 1956); Ruth B. Bordin and Robert M. Warner, "The Library and the Researcher" and "The Library and the General Public," *The Modern Manuscript Library* (New York: Scarecrow Press, 1966); Kenneth Duckett, "Uses of Collections," *Modern Manuscripts: A Practical Manual for Their Management, Care, and Use* (Nashville: American Association for State and Local History, 1975); George Chalou, "Reference," *A Modern Archives Reader: Basic Readings on Archival Theory and Practice* (Washington: National Archives, 1984); Sandra Hinchey and Sigrid McCausland, "Access and Reference Services," *Keeping Archives* (Sydney: Australian Society of Archives, 1987); and David R. Kepley, "Reference Service and Access," *Managing Archives and Archival Institutions* (Chicago: University of Chicago Press, 1988).

A useful collection of essays is Lucille Whalen, ed., *Reference Services in Archives* (New York: Haworth Press, 1986), which provides examples of reference services in a wide variety of settings. It includes, for example, Thomas Wilsted, "Establishing an Image: The Role of Reference Service in a New Archival Program"; Cynthia Swank, "Life in the Fast Lane: Reference in a Business Archives"; and Frank A. Zabrosky, "Researching the Past: An Archivist's Perspective."

In 1939, the ever-prescient Margaret Norton provided one of the earliest and one of the best discussions of reference service in archives, "Archives and Libraries: Reference Work" in *Illinois Libraries* 21 (August 1939): 26-28, reprinted in *Norton on Archives* (Carbondale, Ill.: Southern University Press, 1975), 101-05. A useful history of the evolution of reference service at the National Archives is found in Donald R. McCoy, *The National Archives: America's Ministry of Documents, 1934-1968* (Chapel Hill: University of North Carolina, 1978).

Although written for the novice scholar, Philip C. Brooks, *Research in Archives: The Use of Unpublished Primary Sources* (Chicago: University of Chicago Press, 1969) offers useful insight into reference services in archives. Now dated but useful for a view of the research training of historians is Walter Rundell, Jr., *In Pursuit of American History: Research and Training in the United States* (Norman: University of Oklahoma Press, 1970).

Users of Archives

Systematic exploration of the uses and users of archives is a recent phenomenon; archival reference services rest on largely untested assumptions about users, colored by attitudes and expectations that have evolved through the years. The elitism of the Historical Manuscripts Tradition persisted well into the twentieth century. See, for example, Howard Peckham "Aiding the Scholar in Using Manuscript Collections," *American Archivist* 19 (July 1956): 221-28; and Jean Preston, "Problems in the Use of Manuscripts," *American Archivist* 28 (July 1965): 367-79. In contrast, the Public Archives Tradition, which became dominant in the past fifty years, emphasized reference services to the general public. See for example, Margaret Pierson, "Reference Services in the Indiana State Archives," and W. G. Ormsby, "Reference Service in the Public Archives of Canada," both in *American Archivist* 25 (July 1962): 341-51. These traditions are described by Richard Berner in *Archival Theory and Practice in the United States: A Historical Analysis* (Seattle: University of Washington Press, 1983), which, in spite of its title, is devoted to arrangement and description and only considers reference by implication.

A considerable portion of the literature about archival reference services is found in articles discussing the relationship between the user and the archivist. Users are usually defined as persons who initiate contact with the repository directly, not as the wider public. Users are also typically defined as historians, occasionally as administrators or genealogists. See for example, Frank B. Evans, "The State Archivist and the Academic Researcher," *American Archivist* 26 (July 1963): 319-21; William F. Birdsall, "The Two Sides of the Desk: Archivist and Historian, 1909-1935," *American Archivist* 38 (April 1975): 159-73; and Dale C. Mayer, "The New Social History: Implications for Archivists," *American Archivist* 48 (Fall 1985): 388-99.

Archival users have described their experiences in print. Examples include Philip D. Jordan, "The Scholar and the Archivist," *American Archivist* 31 (January 1968): 57-65; Laurence R. Veysey, "A Scholar's View of University Archives," *College and University Archives: Selected Readings* (Chicago:

Society of American Archivists, 1979), 145-54. Page Putnam Miller, *Developing a Premier National Institution: A Report from the User Community to the National Archives* (Washington: National Coordinating Committee for the Promotion of History, 1989) is a useful recent statement of the viewpoint of scholarly users of the National Archives. Two critical commentaries are Carl M. Brauer, "Researcher Evaluation of Reference Services," *American Archivist* 43 (Winter 1980): 77-79; and Mary N. Speakman, "The User Talks Back," *American Archivist* 47 (Spring 1984): 164-71. Coming to hand as this book goes to press is Ann D. Gordon, *Using the Nation's Documentary Heritage: The Report of the Historical Documents Study* (Washington D.C.: NHPRC, 1992).

In the mid 1980s archivists began to consider what the effects would be if the profession were driven by the needs of users, rather than records. Elsie Freeman, for example, urged archivists to "begin to think of archives administration as client-centered, not materials-centered" in "In the Eye of the Beholder: Archives Administration from the User's Point of View," *American Archivist* 47 (Spring 1984): 111-23 and in "Buying Quarter Inch Holes: Public Support through Results," *Midwestern Archivist* 10 (1985): 89-97. Others who have urged this perspective include Hugh Taylor, *Archival Services and the Concept of The User: A RAMP Study* (Paris: UNESCO, 1984).

See also William L. Joyce, "Archivists and Research Use," *American Archivist* 47 (Spring 1984): 124-33; David Bearman and Richard H. Lytle, "The Power of the Principle of Provenance," *Archivaria* 21 (1985): 14-27; Bruce Dearstyne, "What is the *Use* of Archives? A Challenge for the Profession," *American Archivist* 50 (Winter 1987): 76-87; Planning Group on the Educational Potential of Archives, Committee on Goals and Priorities, *An Action Agenda for the Archival Profession: Institutionalizing the Planning Process* (Chicago: Society of American Archivists, 1988); and Randall C. Jimerson, "Redefining Archival Identity: Meeting User Needs in the Information Society," *American Archivist* 52 (Summer 1989): 332-40.

These and other writers urge the necessity for user studies, although the 1985 SAA Census of Archival Institutions suggests that most archives do not collect even the most rudimentary information about use. See, for example, Richard H. Lytle, "A National Information System for Archives and Manuscript Collections," *American Archivist* 43 (Summer 1980): 423-26; and Lawrence Dowler, "The Role of Use in Defining Archival Practice and Principle: A Research Agenda for the Availability and Use of Records," *American Archivist* 51 (Winter and Spring 1988): 74-86.

Paul Conway has been instrumental in showing archivists the value and practice of user studies, especially in his "Facts and Frameworks: An Approach to Studying the Users of Archives," *American Archivist* 49 (Fall 1986): 393-407. Other useful articles about user studies include Clark Elliott, "Citation Patterns and Documentation for the History of Science: Some Methodological Considerations," *American Archivist* 44 (Spring 1981): 143-50; Fredric Miller, "Use, Appraisal and Research: A Case Study of Social History," *American Archivist* 49 (Fall 1986): 371-92; Bruce H. Bruemmer, "Keeping Track of Reference Use," *MAC Newsletter* (October 1988): 15-18; and David Bearman, "User Presentation Language in Archives," *Archives and Museum Informatics* 3 (Winter 1989-90): 3-7.

A useful compilation of articles on user studies is found in *Midwestern Archivist* 11 (Summer 1986). It includes William J. Maher, "The Use of User Studies"; Jacqueline Goggin, "The Indirect Approach: A Study of Scholarly Users of Black and Women's Organizational Records in the Library of Congress Manuscripts Division"; Roy C. Turnbaugh, "Archival Mission and User Studies"; and Paul Conway, "Research in Presidential Libraries: A User Survey."

Early examples of user studies focusing on traditional academic historical scholars include Margaret Steig, "The Information of [sic] Needs of Historians," *College and Research Libraries* 42 (November 1981): 544-60; and Michael E. Stevens, "The Historian and Archival Finding Aids," *Georgia Archive* 5 (Winter 1977): 64-74. A more recent study is Stephen E. Wiberley, Jr., and William G. Jones, "Patterns of Information Seeking in the Humanities," *College and Research Libraries* 50 (November 1989): 638-45.

The special needs of handicapped users have not been discussed widely in print. See, however, Lance J. Fischer, "The Deaf and Archival Research: Some Problems and Solutions," *American Archivist* 42 (October 1979): 463-64; and Brenda Beasley Kepley, "Archives: Access for the Disabled," *American Archivist* 46 (Winter 1983): 42-51.

Intellectual Aspects of Reference Service

The intellectual functions of reference services in archives, especially the importance of mediation in provenance-based systems, have not been widely explored. Frank Burke succinctly described the indispensable role of the archivist in providing subject access in his deceptively titled, "The Impact of the Specialist on Archives," *College and Research Libraries* 33 (1972): 321-17. Richard Lytle analyzed the two methods of access in "Intellectual Access to Archives: Provenance and Content Indexing Methods of Subject Retrieval," *American Archivist* 43 (Winter 1980: 64-75. These insights were elaborated by Mary Jo Pugh, "The Illusion of Omniscience: Subject Access and the Reference Archivist," *American Archivist* 45 (Winter 1982): 33-44, reprinted in *Modern Archives Reader.* An excellent discussion of the intellectual aspects of the reference interaction in archives is found in American Management Systems, "Methodology for Developing an Expert System for Information Retrieval at the National Archives and Records Administration," (Washington, D. C.: National Archives and Records Administration, 1986).

All reference archivists should read JoAnne Yates, *Control Through Communication: The Rise of System in American Management* (Baltimore: Johns Hopkins University Press, 1989) for its fine discussion of the history of organizational communication, information flows, information technology, and document forms. Also useful is Richard J. Cox, "Bibliography and Reference for the Archivist," *American Archivist* 46 (Spring 1983): 185-87. Provocative and important is David Bearman, *Archival Methods*, Archives and Museum Informatics Report 9 (Pittsburgh: Archives and Museum Informatics, 1989).

William Saffady remains a pioneer in emphasizing the educational role of reference service in archives, "Reference Services to Researchers in Archives," *RQ* (Winter 1974): 139-44.

Improving intellectual access through finding aids has been widely discussed in recent years. See for example, David Bearman and Richard Lytle, "The Power of the Principle of Provenance," *Archivaria* 21 (1985-1986): 14-27; and "Archival Descriptive Standards: Establishing a Process for Their Development and Implementation. Report and Recommendations of the Working Group on Standards for Archival Description." *American Archivist* 52 (Fall 1989): 440-77.

Because automation was first used to improve the production of existing finding aids the impact of automation on reference service is just now beginning to be felt. Most thought-provoking is David Bearman, "Archives and Manuscript Control With Bibliographic Utilities: Opportunities and Challenges," *American Archivist* 52 (Winter 1989): 26-39. See also Nancy Sahli, "National Information Systems and Strategies for Research Use," *Midwestern Archivist* 9 (1984): 5-14; and Avra Michelson, "Description and Reference in the Age of Automation," *American Archivist* 50 (Spring 1987): 192-208.

Interpersonal Aspects

In contrast to the library literature, which is voluminous, there is little published about the interpersonal elements of the reference encounter in archives. The best introduction to this subject is Linda J. Long, "Question Negotiation in the Archival Setting: The Use of Interpersonal Communication Techniques in the Reference Interview," *American Archivist* 52 (Winter 1989): 40-51. An earlier discussion of reference that emphasizes the human element is Robert Rosenthal, "The User and the Used," *Drexel Library Quarterly* (January 1975): 97-105.

Access

Access issues have frequently dominated discussions of reference service in archives. The best source for understanding all legal aspects of access is Gary M. Peterson and Trudy Huskamp Peterson, *Archives and Manuscripts: Law* (Chicago: Society of American Archivists, 1985). The best discussion of the history of access practices at the national level is found in Raymond H. Geselbracht, "The Origins of Restrictions on Access to Personal Papers in the Library of Congress and the National Archives," *American Archivist* 49 (Spring 1986): 142-62. An international perspective is provided in Michel Duchein, *Obstacles to the Access, Use and Transfer of Information from Archives: RAMP Study* (Paris: UNESCO, 1983).

Discussions between archivists and scholars about the issue of access to recent records have produced an extensive bibliography. See for example, *Final Report of the Joint AHA OAH Ad Hoc Committee to Investigate the Charges against the Franklin D. Roosevelt Library and Related Matters* (Washington: American Historical Association, 1970); and Alonzo L. Hamby and Edward Weldon, *Access to Papers of Recent Public Figures: The New Harmony Conference* (Bloomington, Indiana: Organization of American Historians, 1977).

Writing access policies has been considered by Anne Van Camp, "Access Policies for Corporate Archives," *American Archivist* 45 (1982): 296-98; Edie Hedlin, "Access: The Company *vs.* the Scholar," *Georgia Archives* 7 (Spring 1979): 1-9; Phyllis Barr, "Access to Church Records," *Provenance* 1 (1983): 40-48; and "Developing An Access Policy," *Keeping*

Archives (Sydney: Australian Society of Archivists, 1987), 190-98.

Administration of access is considered in Roland Baumann, "Administration of Access in State Archives," *American Archivist* 49 (1986): 349-69; Alice Robbin, "State Archives and Issues of Privacy," *American Archivist* 49 (Spring 1986): 163-75; Harold L. Miller, "Will Access Restrictions Hold up in Court? The FBI's Attempt to Use the Braden Papers at the State Historical Society of Wisconsin," *American Archivist* 52 (Spring 1989): 180-90; James Gregory Bradsher, "Privacy Act Expungements: A Reconsideration," *Provenance* 6 (Spring 1988): 1-25; and Joan Hoff-Wilson, "Access to Restricted Collections: The Responsibility of Professional Historical Organizations," *American Archivist* 46 (Fall 1983): 441-47.

Margaret L. Hedstrom, "Computers, Privacy and Research Access to Confidential Information," *Midwestern Archivist* 6 (1981): 5-18 is useful for newer privacy issues. Student records are considered in Marjorie Rabe Barritt, "The Appraisal of Personally Identifiable Student Records," *American Archivist* 49 (Summer 1986): 263-75; and Charles B. Elston, "University Student Records: Research Use, Private Rights and the Buckley Law," *Midwestern Archivist* 1 (1976): 16-32.

A 1988 publication of the Mid-Atlantic Regional Archives Conference, *Constitutional Issues and Archives,* considered privacy and copyright issues. It included Roland Baumann, "Privacy Act Expungements: A Necessary Evil?"; James Gregory Bradsher, "We Have a Right to Privacy"; and George Chalou, "We Have a Right to Know."

Ethics

Ethics are defined and discussed in "A Code of Ethics for Archivists," *American Archivist* 43 (Summer 1980): 415-18, and accompanying commentary. Ethical issues are further explored in Nancy Lankford, "Ethics and the Reference Archivist," *Midwestern Archivist* 8 (1983): 7-13. A provocative discussion of the ethical dimensions of access issues is found in Elena Danielson, "The Ethics of Access," *American Archivist* 52 (Winter 1989): 52-62. The code is under revision, See *SAA Newsletter* (July 1991).

Administration of Reference Services

The most useful treatment of security is Timothy Walch, *Archives and Manuscripts: Security* (Chicago: Society of American Archivists, 1977). This topic is also explored by Philip Mason, "Archival Security: New Solutions to an Old Problem," *Ameri-*

can Archivist 38 (October 1975): 477-92. The journal *Library and Archives Security* (New York: Haworth Press) is useful for recent developments. See also "Guidelines Regarding Thefts in Libraries," *C & RL News* (March 1988): 159-162; and "ACRL Guidelines for the Security of Rare Book, Manuscript, and Other Special Collections," *C & RL News* (March 1990): 240-244.

Preservation and the administration of reference services is found in Mary Lynn Ritzenthaler, *Archives and Manuscripts: Conservation* (Chicago: Society of American Archivists, 1983); Mary Lynn Ritzenthaler, Gerald J. Munoff, and Margery S. Long, *Administration of Photographic Collections* (Chicago: Society of American Archivists, 1984); and Ritzenthaler, *Preserving Archives and Manuscripts* (Chicago: Society of American Archivists, forthcoming.) The administrative aspects of the initial interview are elaborated in Robert W. Tissing, Jr., "The Orientation Interview in Archival Research," *American Archivist* 47 (Spring 1984): 173-78.

For more detailed treatment of all aspects of reprography, consult Carolyn Hoover Sung, *Archives and Manuscripts: Reprography* (Chicago: Society of American Archivists, 1982). Also noteworthy is Nancy Gwinn, *Preservation Microfilming: A Guide for Librarians and Archivists* (Chicago: American Library Association, 1987). For an introduction to newer copying forms see David Bearman, *Optical Media: Their Implications for Archives and Muse-* ums (Pittsburgh: Archival and Museum Informatics, 1987). An early plea from a user to facilitate photocopying is Walter Rundell, Jr., "To Serve Scholarship," *American Archivist* 30 (October 1967): 547-55.

Promoting the Use of Archives

As seen above, much has been written on the importance of promoting the use of archives in recent years. In addition to those titles is Elsie Freivogel, "Educational Programs: Outreach as an Administrative Function," *American Archivist* 41 (April 1978): 147-53.

A particularly useful contribution towards implementation is Ann E. Pederson, "User Education and Public Relations," *Keeping Archives* (Sydney: Australian Society of Archivists, 1987); also very helpful in implementing education programs is Ann E. Pederson and Gail Farr Casterline, *Archives and Manuscripts: Public Programs* (Chicago: Society of American Archivists, 1982), 39-50. See also *Toward a Usable Past* (Albany: New York State Archives, 1984). Also notable are Elsie Freeman, "Public Programs: What Alice Didn't Say," *SAA Reference, Access, and Outreach Newsletter* 2 (August 1987): 3-4; Joel Wurl, "Methodology as Outreach: A Public Mini-course on Archival Principles and Techniques," *American Archivist* 49 (Spring 1986): 184-86; and Sandra Myres, "Public Program for Archives: Reaching Patrons, Officials, and the Public," *Georgia Archive* 7 (Spring 1979): 10-15.

Appendix 1
ALA-SAA Joint Statement on Access to Original Research Materials in Libraries, Archives, and Manuscript Repositories

1. It is the responsibility of a library, archives, or manuscript repository to make available original research materials in its possession on equal terms of access. Since the accessibility of material depends on knowing of its existence, it is the responsibility of a repository to inform researchers of the collections and archival groups in its custody. This may be accomplished through a card catalog, inventories and other internal finding aids, published guides or reports to the National Union Catalog of Manuscript Collections where appropriate, and the freely offered assistance of staff members, who, however, should not be expected to engage in extended research.

2. To protect and insure the continued accessibility of the material in its custody, the repository may impose several conditions which it should publish or otherwise make known to users.

    a. The repository may limit the use of fragile or unusually valuable materials, so long as suitable reproductions are made available for the use of all researchers.

    b. All materials must be used in accordance with the rules of and under the supervision of the repository. Each repository should publish and furnish to potential researchers its rules governing access and use. Such rules must be equally applied and enforced.

    c. The repository may refuse access to unprocessed materials, so long as such refusal is applied to all researchers.

    d. Normally, a repository will not send research materials for use outside its building or jurisdiction. Under special circumstances a collection or a portion of it may be loaned or placed on deposit with another institution.

    e. The repository may refuse access to an individual researcher who has demonstrated such carelessness or deliberate destructiveness as to endanger the safety of the material.

    f. As a protection to its holdings, a repository may reasonably require acceptable identification of persons wishing to use its materials, as well as a signature indicating they have read a statement defining the policies and regulations of the repository.

3. Each repository should publish or otherwise make available to researchers a suggested form of cita-
tion crediting the repository and identifying items within its holdings for later reference. Citations to copies of materials in other repositories should include the location of the originals, if known.

4. Whenever possible a repository should inform a researcher about known copyrighted material, the owner or owners of the copyrights, and the researcher's obligations with regard to such material.

5. A repository should not deny access to materials to any person or persons, nor grant privileged or exclusive use of materials to any person or persons, nor conceal the existence of any body of material from any researcher, unless required to do so by law, donor, or purchase stipulations.

6. A repository should, whenever possible, inform a researcher of parallel research by other individuals using the same materials. With the written acquiescence of those other individuals, a repository may supply their names upon request.

7. Repositories are committed to preserving manuscript and archival materials and to making them available for research as soon as possible. At the same time, it is recognized that every repository has certain obligations to guard against unwarranted invasion of personal privacy and to protect confidentiality in its holdings in accordance with the law and that every private donor has the right to impose reasonable restrictions upon his papers to protect privacy or confidentiality for a reasonable period of time.

    a. It is the responsibility of the repository to inform researchers of the restrictions which apply to individual collections or archival groups.

    b. The repository should discourage donors from imposing unreasonable restrictions and should encourage a specific time limitation on such restrictions as are imposed.

    c. The repository should periodically reevaluate restricted material and work toward the removal of restrictions when they are no longer required.

8. A repository should not charge fees for making available the materials in its holdings. However, reasonable fees may be charged for the copying of material or for the provision of special services or facilities not provided to all researchers.

Appendix 2
Statement on the Reproduction of Manuscripts and Archives for Reference Use

1. It is the responsibility of a library, archives, or manuscript repository to assist researchers by making or having made reproductions of any material in its possession, for research purposes, subject to certain conditions. Manuscript and archival materials may be reproduced if:
   (a) The condition of the originals will permit such reproduction.
   (b) The originals have no gift, purchase, or legal restrictions on reproduction.

2. In the interest of making research collections more generally available, the orderly microfilming of archives and entire manuscript collections, together with appropriate guides, is to be encouraged, within the available resources of the repository.

3. The price of reproductions shall be set by the repository, which should endeavor to keep charges to a minimum.

4. Copies should be made for reference use as follows:
   (a) Repositories which permit their manuscript and archival holdings to be reproduced in whole or in part must specify before the copies are made what restrictions, if any, have been placed on the use or further reproduction of copies.
   (b) Repositories may require that purchasers agree in writing to abide by any restrictions.
   (c) All reproductions should identify the source of the original manuscript collection or archival record group.

5. The repository should inform the researcher:
   (a) When and under what conditions permission to make extensive direct quotation from or to print in full any reproduction must be obtained from the institution owning the originals.
   (b) That in the case of material under copyright, the right to quote or print, beyond fair use, must also be obtained by the researcher from the copyright owner.
   (c) That the researcher assumes legal reponsibility for observing common law literary rights, property rights, and libel laws.
   (d) Of known retention of literary rights.

6. A repository may decline to furnish reproductions when fulfilling mail requests requires subjective criteria for selection of material to be duplicated or the commitment of an unreasonable amount of staff time for extended research to identify the material.

7. In cases when researchers request the reproduction of large amounts of material which they have identified in the course of their research, the repository may prescribe a preferred method of copying (i.e., microfilm vs. Xerox) and may provide for a reasonable time period in which to produce the copies.

Appendix 3
Copyright Act, Title 17 of the United States Code

Sections 106, 107, and 108

§ 106. Exclusive rights in copyrighted works

Subject to sections 107 through 118, the owner of copyright under this title has the exclusive rights to do and to authorize any of the following:

(1) to reproduce the copyrighted work in copies or phonorecords;

(2) to prepare derivative works based upon the copyrighted work;

(3) to distribute copies or phonorecords of the copyrighted work to the public by sale or other transfer of ownership, or by rental, lease, or lending;

(4) in the case of literary, musical, dramatic, and choreographic works, pantomimes, and motion pictures and other audiovisual works, to perform the copyrighted work publicly; and

(5) in the case of literary, musical, dramatic, and choreographic works, pantomimes, and pictorial, graphic, or sculptural works, including the individual images of a motion picture or other audiovisual work, to display the copyrighted work publicly.

§ 107. Limitations on exclusive rights: Fair use

Notwithstanding the provisions of section 106, the fair use of a copyrighted work, including such use by reproduction in copies or phonorecords or by any other means specified by that section, for purposes such as criticism, comment, news reporting, teaching (including multiple copies for classroom use), scholarship, or research, is not an infringement of copyright. In determining whether the use made of a work in any particular case is a fair use the factors to be considered shall include—

(1) the purpose and character of the use, including whether such use is of a commercial nature or is for nonprofit educational purposes;

(2) the nature of the copyrighted work;

(3) the amount and substantiality of the portion used in relation to the copyrighted work as a whole; and

(4) the effect of the use upon the potential market for or value of the copyrighted work.

§ 108. Limitations on exclusive rights: Reproduction by libraries and archives

(a) Notwithstanding the provisions of section 106, it is not an infringement of copyright for a library or archives, or any of its employees acting within the scope of their employment, to reproduce no more than one copy or phonorecord of a work, or to distribute such copy or phonorecord, under the conditions specified by this section, if—

(1) the reproduction or distribution is made without any purpose of direct or indirect commercial advantage;

(2) the collections of the library or archives are (i) open to the public, or (ii) available not only to researchers affiliated with the library or archives or with the institution of which it is a part, but also to other persons doing research in a specialized field; and

(3) the reproduction or distribution of the work includes a notice of copyright.

(b) The rights of reproduction and distribution under this section apply to a copy or phonorecord of an unpublished work duplicated in facsimile form solely for purposes of preservation and security or for deposit for research use in another library or archives of the type described by clause (2) of subsection (a), if the copy or phonorecord reproduced is currently in the collections of the library or archives.

(c) The right of reproduction under this section applies to a copy or phonorecord of a published work duplicated in facsimile form solely for the purpose of replacement of a copy or phonorecord that is damaged, deteriorating, lost, or stolen, if the library or archives has, after a reasonable effort, determined that an unused replacement cannot be obtained at a fair price.

(d) The rights of reproduction and distribution under this section apply to a copy, made from the collection of a library or archives where the user makes his or her request or from that of another library or archives, of no more than one article or other contribution to a copyrighted collection or periodical issue, or to a copy or phonorecord of a small part of any other copyrighted work, if—

(1) the copy or phonorecord becomes the property of the user, and the library or archives has had no notice that the copy or phonorecord

would be used for any purpose other than private study, scholarship, or research; and

(2) the library or archives displays prominently, at the place where orders are accepted, and includes on its order form, a warning of copyright in accordance with requirements that the Register of Copyrights shall prescribe by regulation.

(e) The rights of reproduction and distribution under this section apply to the entire work, or to a substantial part of it, made from the collection of a library or archives where the user makes his or her request or from that of another library or archives, if the library or archives has first determined, on the basis of a reasonable investigation, that a copy or phonorecord of the copyrighted work cannot be obtained at a pair price, if—

(1) the copy or phonorecord becomes the property of the user, and the library or archives has had no notice that the copy or phonorecord would be used for any purpose other than private study, scholarship, or research; and

(2) the library or archives displays prominently, at the place where orders are accepted, and includes on its order form, a warning of copyright in accordance with requirements that the Register of Copyrights shall prescribe by regulation.

(f) Nothing in this section—

(1) shall be construed to impose liability for copyright infringement upon a library or archives or its employees for the unsupervised use of reproducing equipment located on its premises: *Provided,* That such equipment displays a notice that the making of a copy may be subject to the copyright law;

(2) excuses a person who uses such reproducing equipment or who requests a copy or phonorecord under subsection (d) from liability for copyright infringement for any such act, or for any later use of such copy or phonorecord, if it exceeds fair use as provided by section 107;

(3) shall be construed to limit the reproduction and distribution by lending of a limited number of copies and excerpts by a library or archives of an audiovisual news program, subject to clauses (1), (2), and (3) of subsection (a); or

(4) in any way affects the right of fair use as provided by section 107, or any contractual obligations assumed at any time by the library

or archives when it obtained a copy or phonorecord of a work in its collections.

(g) The rights of reproduction and distribution under this section extend to the isolated and unrelated reproduction or distribution of a single copy or phonorecord of the same material on separate occasions, but do not extend to cases where the library or archives, or its employee—

(1) is aware or has substantial reason to believe that it is engaging in the related or concerted reproduction or distribution of multiple copies or phonorecords of the same material, whether made on one occasion or over a period of time, and whether intended for aggregate use by one or more individuals or for separate use by the individual members of a group; or

(2) engages in the systematic reproduction or distribution of single or multiple copies or phonorecords of material described in subsection (d): *Provided,* That nothing in this clause prevents a library or archives from participating in interlibrary arrangements that do not have, as their purpose or effect, that the library or archives receiving such copies or phonorecords for distribution does so in such aggregate quantities as to substitute for a subscription to or purchase of such work.

(h) The rights of reproduction and distribution under this section do not apply to a musical work, a pictorial, graphic or sculptural work, or a motion picture or other audiovisual work other than an audiovisual work dealing with news, except that no such limitation shall apply with respect to rights granted by subsections (b) and (c), or with respect to pictorial or graphic works published as illustrations, diagrams, or similar adjuncts to works of which copies are reproduced or distributed in accordance with subsections (d) and (e).

(i) Five years from the effective date of this Act, and at five-year intervals thereafter, the Register of Copyrights, after consulting with representatives of authors, book and periodical publishers, and other owners of copyrighted materials, and with representatives of library users and librarians, shall submit to the Congress a report setting forth the extent to which this section has achieved the intended statutory balancing of the rights of creators, and the needs of users. The report should also describe any problems that may have arisen, and present legislative or other recommendations, if warranted.

Appendix 4
Access Policies and Reference Services

Principles. "The archives must provide opportunity for research in the records it holds. The archives should be open for research use on a regular and stated schedule. It should provide adequate space and facilities for research use and should make its records available on equal terms of access to all users who should abide by its rules and procedures. Any restrictions on access should be defined in writing and should be carefully observed.

The archives should provide information about its holdings and assist and instruct users in their use. Staff members familiar with the holdings and capable of making informed decisions about legal and ethical consideration affecting reference work should be available to assist readers. The archives should report its holdings to appropriate publications so that potential users may know of their existence. The archives should assist users by providing reproductions of materials in its possession whenever possible."

Amplification. Any restrictions on access should be defined in writing and should be carefully observed. There should be regular and systematic review of restrictions to determine when they expire, and prompt opening of material upon expiration of restrictions.

An archives should protect and preserve materials used, including loans and materials used in reading rooms, so that they may survive for future use. It should keep records of the identity of all users and their use of materials to assess patterns of use, to trace previous research paths, and to support replevin of alienated materials. Rules and procedures for use should protect historical materials and legitimate interests of the archives. They should be stated clearly and posted for examination by all users. They should not unduly encumber access to sources.

An archives should comply with applicable laws, especially those related to proprietary rights (such as copyright), privacy and confidentiality, and freedom of information. An archives has a responsibility to inform users of laws and governmental or institutional regulations that affect their research.

YES   NO   N/A

_____   _____   _____   1. Does the archives maintain hours of service on a regular and posted schedule?

_____   _____   _____   2. Are the number of hours reasonably adequate for anticipated use?

_____   _____   _____   3. Does the archives have a written policy on access?

_____   _____   _____   4. Is the access policy equitable and consistent with the SAA Statement on Access?

_____   _____   _____   5. Does the policy clearly define who may use the facility?

_____   _____   _____   6. Are the records of restrictions well-maintained, clear, and easily and equitably administered?

_____   _____   _____   7. Is there a systematic procedure for periodic review of restrictions and prompt opening of materials after restrictions expire?

——— —	———	——— —

8. Is there an adequate plan for deciding whether an unprocessed or partially processed collection shall be made available for research?

9. Is the policy regarding loans equitable, and easily administered?

10. Are loaned records adequately protected?

11. Does the archives keep adequate records of materials loaned?

12. Does the archives provide for readers written guidelines containing information about policies affecting research use, such as access policies, rules for use of materials, security rules, sample citations, photocopy, policies, copyright provisions, and other specific information?

13. Are the rules and procedures adequate to control and protect materials, provide a proper atmosphere for research, and yet not unduly impede access to materials?

14. Is the space provided for researchers (the reading room) adequate?

15. Is the reading room appropriately equipped for the records to be examined?

16. Is it adequately staffed?

17. Is staff supervision and surveillance sufficient to provide necessary assistance and to prevent theft or damage, including potential dangers from copying documents?

18. Does the archives answer written requests for information about its holdings?

19. Does the archives answer telephone requests for information about its holdings?

20. Are there appropriate guides to the archives?

21. Does the archives make finding aids available to readers?

22. Does the archives regularly report holdings and new accessions to major catalogues such as NUCMC and/or enter descriptive information about record groups and collections into on-line catalogues and databases?

23. Are the records of reference service adequate to permit analysis of reference needs, to provide protection in case of theft or abuse, and to permit planning for and evaluation of reference services?

24. Does the archives have a policy on informing readers of parallel research?
25. Is an adequate reference collection accessible?
26. Does the archives provide copying services to researchers?
27. Is the copying service convenient and are its charges/fees appropriate?
28. Are records adequately protected from harm during copying?
29. Does the archives refuse to provide copies when the copy process risks damage to the original?
30. Are staff members who deal with researchers well-informed about laws affecting research, especially copyright, privacy, and freedom of information laws?
31. Do staff members inform users of the implications of these laws for their research as appropriate?

Archives Planning and Assessment Workbook (Chicago: Society of American Archivists, 1989), 45-47.

Index

Academic libraries, 5

Access (*See also* Access policy; Intellectual access; Legal access; Physical access; Restricted access), 5, 17-18, 53, 102-3; archival responsibilities, 55-56; automation and, 105; bibliographic works on, 112; classified information and, 59; concepts, 55-56; confidentiality and, 55-59, 63-64; copies and, 86; copyright and, 119-20; deeds of gift and, 56-59, 61-62, 64; definitions, 55-56; description and, 6; equality of, 55-56, 59-61, 64; ethical aspects, 56, 59, 63-64, 112; guidelines, 55-56; privacy and, 55-59, 64, 106; privileged communications, 57, 63; right to know and, 55-56, 58-59, 64; transmittal documents and, 56-59, 61, 64

Accession: copies, 86

Access policy, 49, 53, 55-56, 59-60; acquisitions and, 59-60, 64; administration, 56, 59-61, 64; and use of information, 62; citation and, 62-63; conflicts of interest, 64; copies and, 65, 91; copyright and, 62; creator and, 60; defining, 59-60; denial of access, 60, 62; donor and, 60; fees and, 60-62; intellectual access and, 60-61, 64; legal access and, 64; legal aspects, 60; loans and, 64-65, 90-91; mission statement and, 102; physical access and, 62, 65, 71-76; processing and, 59-60, 64; purpose, 4-5; publication and, 62; reference and, 61, 64, 121-23; restricted access and, 61; SAA and, 59-60, 63-64, 115; security and, 62, 64, 95; service aspects, 61, 64; staff use and, 63-64; users and, 55-56, 60

Acquisition: access policy and, 59-60, 64; copyright and, 62

Archives (*See also* Archivists; Manuscripts repositories; Outreach), 3-4, 13; academic archives, students and, 19-21; compared to libraries, 3-4; evaluation, 93, 98-101; government archives, 4-5; information about, 25, 28, 50, 69, 71; information about holdings, 105; information about records creators, supplying, 38-39; information from holdings, supplying, 36-39; mission statement, 102; planning, 104; public archives tradition and, 5; referrals, 37-39; state archives, 5; use of, 4-5, 12-13, 102-4; value of, 9, 11, 65, 93, 97-98, 102-4; volunteers, 9

Archivists (*See also* Reference archivists), 15; preservation and, 68; research and, 63-64; security and, 66

Arrangement, 25; access and, 6; question negotiation and, 43-44; reference service organization and, 93; research and, 43-44; technology and, 105-6

Automation: and access, 105; finding aids and, 105; intellectual access and, 105; legal access and, 106-7; physical access and, 76; reference and, 97, 105-7; registration and, 76; retrieval of materials and, 76; user studies and, 100

Bibliographic databases. *See* Databases

Confidentiality: access and, 55-59, 63-64

Conservation, 68

Copies (*See also* Microfilm and microfilming), 79-81, 113; access and, 86; access policy and, 65, 85-86, 89, 91; accessioning and, 86; contracting out, 89; copyright and, 81-82, 85; costs and fees, 86, 89; exhibits and, 79-80, 87; instructions, 86-87; legal uses, 79-80; limits, 85-86; mail or phone requests, 86; order forms, 86-88; photographs, 83; preservation and, 79-80, 85-86; procedures, 85-89; publication and, 79; reference and, 89; research and, 79; SAA guidelines and, 85-86; security and, 88-89; staff, copying by, 85-86, 89; standards, 89; types, 80-81, 88-89

Copyright: access and, 119-20; access policy and, 62; acquisition and, 62; copies and, 81-82, 85; fair use and, 82, 84; finding aids and, 62; interpretation of law, 83-85; notices, 83, 85, 88; ownership, 81-82; protection, scope, 81-83; publication and, 62; rights, limitation, 82-83; transfer, 82; user agreements and, 83, 85-86, 88

Databases, 25, 31; arrangement and, 105-6; description and, 31-32, 105-6; in-house databases, 25, 28; libraries and, 34, 36; MARC AMC and, 34-36; MARC VM and, 32; Online Computer Library Center (OCLC), 19, 36; question negotiation and, 43-44; reference and, 105; Research Libraries Information Network (RLIN), 19, 34-36

Description, 25; access and, 6; collective description, 30-31; content-indexing and, 30-31; nontextual materials, 32; provenance and, 28-31; reference service organization and, 93; security and, 65; standards, 31-31; subject surveys, 34; technology and, 105-6; user studies and, 100

Directories, 25-28, 32

Disaster planning, 68

Electronic records. *See* Machine-readable records

Exhibits: care of materials and, 90; copies and, 79-80, 87; loans and, 90

Family Educational and Privacy Rights Act (FERPA), 57

Films, 17; copies of, 79

Finding aids (*See also* Intellectual access), 6, 16, 24, 25, 28; access policy and, 61; and copyright, 62; automation and, 105; calendars, 30-31; catalogs and cataloging, 25, 28, 30-34, 105; guides, 25-26, 28, 30-34; indexes and indexing, 25, 28, 30-31, 105; inventories, 25, 28, 30-31, 36, 105; manuscript repositories, 30-31; physical access and, 69, 71; question negotiation and, 43-44; registers, 25, 28, 31, 105; reference service and, 39; vertical files, 38

Genealogy and genealogists: archives and, 22-23; reference and, 23

Historical societies, 5

Intellectual access (*See also* Finding aids), 6, 9, 24-39, 91; access policy and, 60-61, 64; automation and, 105; bibliographic works, 111-12; types of, 25; user education and, 14

Legal access, 6, 9, 24, 55-60, 91; access policy and, 64; automation and, 106-7; copyright and, 119-20

Libraries: bibliographic databases and, 34, 36; holdings, compared to archives, 3, 4; research libraries, 5

Loans, 89-91; access policy and, 64-65, 90-91; administrative use, 90; agreements, 91; exhibits and, 90; procedures, 90-91; research, 90; substitutes for, 89-90

Machine-readable records: physical access, 76, 106; reference and, 76-77, 106

Manuscript repositories, 3-5; description, content-indexing and, 30-31; finding aids, 30-31

Manuscripts, 3

MARC AMC: databases and, 34-36; description process and, 31-32

MARC VM, 32

Microfilm and microfilming, 79-81; preservation and, 80; procedure, 80, 88-89; standards, 80

National Archives and Records Administration (NARA), 5, 59

National Endowment for the Humanities (NEH), 5

National Historical Publications and Records Commission (NHPRC), 5

National Union Catalog of Manuscript Collections (NUCMC), 32-34

Nontextual materials, 32

Online public access systems. *See* Databases

Original order, 6, 29, 32, 66

Outreach (*See also* Exhibits), 9, 11, 28, 104; bibliographic works, 113; evaluation, 53; planning, 50-52; reference and, 7-8; scholarship and, 19; types of, 50-52

Photographs: citation and, 62-63; copies, 79, 81, 83, 88-89; copyright, 83; description and, 32; standards, 88

Physical access (*See also* Research room), 6, 9, 24, 76-77, 91; access policy and, 60, 62, 65, 71-76; administration, 72, 106; automation and, 76; copies, 77; daily log, 72; equipment, 66, 68, 71; finding aids and, 69, 71; interpersonal aspects, 72; loans, 77; machine-readable records, 76, 106; preservation and, 66, 68-69, 76-77; procedures, 65-67, 73-76; request forms, 74-76; retrieval of materials, 74-76, 106; security and, 65-66, 69-71, 73-77; technology and, 105-7; user identification and registration, 70-73, 106

Preservation, 95; copies and, 79-80, 85-86; microfilming and, 80; physical access and, 66, 68-69, 76-77; reference and, 68, 98, 113; research room design and, 69; user education and, 68, 76

Privacy: access and, 55-59, 64, 106

Procedures manuals: physical access and, 65-67

Processing: access policy and, 59-60, 64

Provenance, 6, 7, 32, 66

Question negotiation: arrangement and, 43-44; elements of, 41-45; finding aids and, 43-44; interpersonal dynamics and, 47; organization archives and, 43-44; process, 41-45, 48; reference interview and, 41-45; user studies and, 100

Reference archivists, 98, 100; advocacy and communication, 97; and provenance-based description systems, 30; evaluation, 101-2, 104; para-professional staff, 95; qualifications, 94-95; scheduling, 97; tracking systems, 97; training, 93-95

Reference interview (*See also* Question negotiation), 9, 41, 45, 72; interpersonal dynamics and, 46-48; location, 47-48; mail and telephone inquiries, 49-50; policy and, 49

Reference services (*See also* Copies; Outreach; Reference archivists; Reference interview; Research room), 6-8, 91; access policy and, 61, 64, 121-23; administration, 6, 8, 41, 45, 48-49, 53, 112-13; automation and, 97, 105-7;

bibliographies, 109-13; confidentiality, 95; copies and, 77, 79, 89, 95, 113, 117; data collection, 93; ethical aspects, 8-9; evaluation, 98, 100-2, 104; exit interview, 45, 48, 49; factual questions, 17; finding aids and, 39; intellectual access and, 6-8, 91; interpersonal aspects, 6, 8, 45-48, 53, 94-95, 110, 112; interpretive questions, 16, 18; loans and, 76-77, 79, 89, 95; machine-readable records, 76-77, 106; management, 95-98; orientation, 21, 51-52; organization, 93-95, 98, 104; parent institution and, 14-16, 20, 37; planning, 14, 95; policy, 8-9, 37, 53, 55, 64, 95; preservation and, 95, 98, 113; privacy, 95; procedures manuals, 95-96; quality, 98; ready reference questions, 14; records management and, 95-96; referrals to other sources, 38-39; registration, 96, 100; request forms, 96; research and, 6-7, 36-38, 95; security and, 98, 112; service levels, 95; time management, 96-97; tools, 25-26, 38, 69, 71; value of, 106-7

Research (*See also* Reference; Research room; Users): and archives, purpose of, 4; archivists and, 63-64; levels of, 95

Researchers. *See* Users

Research room, 91; automation and, 106; design, 69, 71; personal materials in, 73-74; preservation and, 69; reference works in, 69, 71; security and, 69; supervision, 69

Restricted access, 17-18, 55, 56; donor agreements and, 58; policy and, 61; screening records, 58, 61, 64; screening users, 58; withdrawal of items, 58-59, 61

Security, 8, 49, 65-66; access policy and, 62, 64, 95; bibliographic works on, 112-13; copies and, 88-89; daily log and, 72; description, 65; interpersonal aspects, 66; original order and, 66; physical access and, 65-66, 69-71, 73-77; provenance and, 66; reference and, 98; research room, 69; staff training and, 66, 68; storage and, 65; user registration and, 70-73, 106

Society of American Archivists (SAA), 5; access policy, 59-60, 63-64, 115; copies, guidelines, 85-86

Sound tapes: description and, 32

Storage: security and, 65

User education (*See also* Outreach), 6-9, 14, 20, 24, 39, 97; access policy and, 62, 64; automation and, 105-6; bibliographies, 113; citation, 62-63; genealogists, 23; general public, 21-22; handling of materials, 68, 75; parent institution and, 15-16; research skills and, 45; students, 20-21

Users (*See also* Outreach; User education; User studies): access policy and, 55-56, 60; bibliographic information, 110-11; constituencies, 14-24, 24, 28, 71; daily log, 72; factual questions, 13, 15, 37; identification, 71-73, 106; interpretative questions, 13-14, 37; needs of, 11-14; registration, 70-73, 76, 106; research methodologies and, 18; statistics, 71; types of, 14-23

User studies, 11, 13, 93, 98-99, 110-11; and potential users, 100-101; automation and, 100; description and, 100; methods, 103-4; planning and, 104; purpose, 103; types, 103; use of, 103-4